BCOT

# Understanding the Sports Process

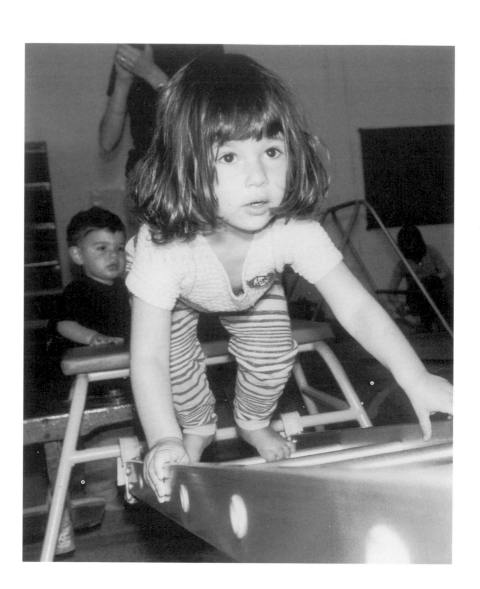

# EFFECTIVE COACHING FOR CHILDREN

*Understanding the Sports Process*

## Misia Gervis and John Brierley

CROWOOD

First published in 1999 by
The Crowood Press Ltd
Ramsbury, Marlborough
Wiltshire SN8 2HR

**British Library Cataloguing in Publication Data**

A catalogue record for this book is available from the British Library.

ISBN  1 86126 137 3

**Dedication**
This book is dedicated to our respective children Kiya, Mitchell, Connor
and Scott.

Throughout this book, 'he', 'him' and 'his' have been used as neutral
pronous and as such refer to both males and females.

The diagrams on p.36 are reproduced with the permission of Stanley
Thornes Publishers Ltd from *Teaching Children to Think* by Robert Fisher,
first published in 1992.

The diagram on p.115 is reproduced by permission from A.V. Carron,
1982, 'Cohesiveness in sports groups: interpretations and
considerations', *Journal of Sport Psychology*, 4 (2): 131.

Printed and bound in Great Britain by J W Arrowsmith, Bristol

# Contents

# Acknowledgements

We would like to thank a number of people who have helped in a variety of ways in the production of this book. We thank you all in no particular order; all the contributions have been invaluable. So here goes: thanks to David for all the wonderful photographs; they have really made the difference. Thanks to all the children, coaches and parents of Hendon Gymnastics Club; we hope you like the result! All the photographs were taken with the kind co-operation of Barnet Council who let us have access to the facility free of charge, and special thanks to Barry Martin who helped arrange the whole thing. We would also like to thank Sharon Clough-Todd for her invaluable contribution on the last chapter – cheers; your words made all the difference.

I would also like to thank some very special gymnasts with whom I have had the privilege to work: Aicha, Nikki and Natalie: you always presented me with a challenge, but with it came inspiration. You have taught me many things – I hope I can pass some of them on. Thank you to my close friends and family, especially my mother: you are a hard act to follow. Finally I would like to thank someone who has taught and shown me so much: you have always provided me with support and inspiration, and I thank you for now and always: Misia.

I would like to thank my parents for their support during my early involvement in sport, and to my coach Terry Torpey for his advice and enthusiasm as I aspired to higher levels. Finally I should like to thank my wife Jackie, without whom this book would have remained an unfinished project: John.

# Foreword

After early successes in football, I opted for the easier life of a decathlete!
My desire to be in as much control of my improvement as a sportsman as
possible was linked to a commitment to work harder than my rivals. Both
of these led me to believe that Athletics was the best vehicle for my tal-
ents. These qualities, and my competitive mentality, helped me to achieve
my goals but I have sometimes wondered what might have happened if I
had chosen a different sport. Since moving out of the competitive arena,
I have considered how we could make this process of sports selection simpler so that children's physical abilities are initially linked with sports that
experts suggest better suit them. It was in connection with a pilot programme for my Sport iD concept that I recently worked with John
Brierley.

I am delighted to endorse this new book which aims to help all those
in a position to give children a positive introduction to sport. With the
development of the child as its central theme, it provides concrete ideas
on what are the best activities to choose for young children and who is
best placed to lead and support them as they learn. It looks at ways of
increasing the mutual support between coaches, parents and teachers so
that children can make greater progress in the middle school years than is
sometimes the case at present. This progresses to consider the transition
to training, the development of talent in sport and coping with confidence
in competitive situations during adolescence. As such it provides the type
of blueprint necessary to fully understand the process of child development through sport for the next generation. It may be the type of practical guidance that could make the difference for some children.

P.S. If you only take one thing out of this book and into your homes and
classrooms it should be that sport is fun at whatever level it is played.
Fun for everyone but most fun for its participants.

Daley Thompson
World, Olympic, European and Commonwealth Decathlon Champion

# Introduction

Sport is a more popular and integral feature of our society than ever before, the massive media coverage that it receives reflecting the importance it is now given in the lives of those who have enjoyed satisfying experiences through involvement. Playing and spectating can bring a real sense of belonging and achievement, as well as the more documented benefits of mental health and physical fitness — indeed, so much so that fond memories often lead us to consider ways in which our children may benefit from play and participation when the time is right. The opportunities for involvement have never been greater — but at the same time this abundant choice can also cloud those important factors which relate to children.

## The Role of the Parent

Children need their own unique support structure of immediate family, social environment and school. They may also need someone involved in their chosen interest (which in our case is physical activity) to stimulate their senses during formative years. Together, such a collection of potential supporters will undoubtedly best serve the needs of the child. As the 'line managers' of their offspring, it is the parents who are expected to take the lead in forming such a team, and undoubtedly this is often the case in relation to home and school selection. But can parents provide meaningful experience in areas such as physical control of the body, appropriate movement experience, and skill learning? Do they know which activities are best suited to young children, or how to recognise when children are ready to cope with new pursuits?

Sometimes their decision is a reaction to peer pressure or to current vogues, sometimes it is influenced by constraints on quality time together as a family unit. Parents usually make decisions about activity selection on the basis of their participation interests, the local facilities and the complexities of transportation, rather than choosing what would be most beneficial to the children. Questions of who is best placed to provide the chosen experience also tend to dwell on qualification issues rather than on philosophy or principles. This is not the parents' fault, as the majority of information regarding early childhood activity does not often compare the values of contrasting experience, or it is written in literature which is read more by researchers than by parents or coaches. This is why practical information based on research into growth, function and early learning is needed.

## The Role of the Teacher

Those who do have some formal training in child development are certainly better placed to understand this momentous process of change. Teachers and nursery nurses are given an introduction to the physical, mental, social and emotional changes that can be expected in early childhood, during their college courses. However, many of the practical experiences associated with normal development are limited to fine manipulative tasks and activities, with no particularly sport-related emphasis. A teacher's belief in the value of whole body movement control, and his use of a wide range of modified sporting equipment, will have evolved from a number of unrelated factors: for instance his interest in sport, his confidence as an activity leader, or simply the budget constraints of the situation, will all influence the emphasis inherent in his teaching.

On 'In Service' courses, primary teachers are often keen to pick up practical ideas for organizing and teaching; they may also make links with agencies who promote specific child-centred approaches to sports introduction. One consequence of this is that it becomes necessary to consider which activities are most appropriate at a particular age, and which community-based projects, such as Tumble Tots Gym, might be recommended from an educational premise.

The coaches of these clubs are often in a similar situation in having part, if not all, of the underpinning knowledge relating to children and sport. Whilst they may not have the formally acquired generic knowledge of child development, they do have considerable experience and sports-specific know-how. They do the same introductory work in sport as their colleagues in other sectors, and they are often based at the same sports centres and community clubs. Perhaps this is a good opportunity to look at their professional routeway in order to assess their respective contribution.

## The Role of the Professional Coach

Coaching is a well established activity, but only a recently evolving profession in this country. Its origins can be traced back to Oxbridge teams and professional sport in the latter part of last century; however, it was only latterly that its development was given renewed impetus, as a response to the success of the Soviet Union team at the 1952 Olympics. The development of a professional coaching network, often where the best coaches were deliberately paired with the more talented young children, provided the desired standard. Even so, twenty years of limited improvement in this country passed before targeted sports facilities expanded to the extent that a new generation of sports coaches was needed. Parents, teachers and former participants were recruited, and later were encouraged to gain initial qualifications through their governing body.

Many of these courses focused heavily upon the correct technical models, rules and training regimes, and whilst this provided a sound knowledge base, it often did little to address the needs of the learner. However, in the last decade this imbalance has been addressed, and the profession has moved on to the extent that over 250,000 coaches are now active, many with current vocational qualifications, working alongside teachers in school situations. Their personal development is much more individually tailored — although this may not always be a good thing: whilst they have relevant and valuable experience in assisting performers to improve in sport, they may have less experience in introducing activity to wide ranges of participant abilities. Coming to terms with the ethos of the school in which they may work on a part-time basis can also take time.

## A Tripartite system

It would appear that all three groups have a great deal to offer the developing child in physical activity and sport, especially if they work in unison. Parents, teachers and coaches have key roles to play in both a leading and a supporting sense, and there is sufficient evidence from other countries that such collaboration does work.

However, such a way of working may be a relatively new concept to some, and would need time to establish itself. The advantage of such a tripartite system is that the process of drawing on a wider base of support is the norm right from the initial years, and this might mean that some of the problems that coaches experience with parents, and vice versa, are less of an issue. It may also enable children to become used to working with different people with skills and styles best suited to their particular role. This may be important in a society where the value of children working more equably with male and female figures has been reported.

The second important premise for this book is that any child is involved in a developmental transition towards adulthood, and this involves growth and the maturation of bodily systems, and the overall development which results from this. Because this happens in a particular way, dependent on hereditary and environmental factors, it is useful to see it as a process different to all others. Adopting such a viewpoint enables us to identify children's readiness as the most important cue for introducing appropriate activity; it also indicates that an individual's process of development in sport should not necessarily be hampered by overmuch reference to chronological age. When things are done is relevant, but is less important than the order in which they should be introduced. It is also an approach which may appear to sit more comfortably with individualized coaching methods — although there can be little doubt that it is also central to individual performers within teams. Essentially it is to be advocated that such activities are selected as are best suited to the needs and the developmental stage of the individual child. The child is thus fundamentally at the centre of a supportive group which combines the gifts and abilities of parents, coaches and teachers in a more integrated way.

# PART ONE
# THE EARLY YEARS

*Taking part in sport can begin before a child is a year old, and whilst it is recognized that this might be classed as physical activity rather than sport, it is nevertheless where children's sporting lives can begin. This section explores a variety of areas from the parent and coach perspective.*

*This section examines the key issues for sport for the under-5s and initially includes an investigation into growth, function, maturation, abilities and skills. The section further introduces areas not normally associated with sports development, but nonetheless critical for a holistic view of the opportunities for the under-5s. These include cognitive development, creativity through physical socialization. It concludes by addressing the practicalities of helping children to become more physically literate by considering good practice, home-based activity and using the playground.*

# CHAPTER ONE

# From Little Acorns

This chapter aims to outline the physical processes that constitute normal development for children between the ages of one and seven years. This pattern of growth, maturity and functional change needs to be fully understood so that the readiness of the child becomes the key factor in activity selection.

## Changes In Physical Apperance

There is no doubt that a child's expected rate of growth to the age of seven is only marginally less impressive, in terms of both amount and velocity, than during either pregnancy or the thirty months during puberty. However, during both these periods the child is either protected from its external environment or has considerable physical control over it. Therefore it is the early years which appear to impose arguably the biggest challenge to children, in that much of their energy is devoted to intense purposeful activity at the same time as they are growing and gaining weight. This may account for some children needing regular naps, and even appearing to grow during them! Whilst changes in stature are clear to see, particularly to intermittent observers, what of the specific milestones?

### The Prenatal Period

During the nine month prenatal period the embryo develops into a foetus with remarkable speed. It has been estimated that from a single cell beginning, the unborn baby grows an average 47cm (19in), which equates to a mass of thirty trillion cells. This represents about 27 per cent of its average final stature for a man, and 29 per cent for a woman. Babies are expected to gain 3.4kg (7.5lb) during the forty-week *in utero* period. After this phenomenal start the growth rate does dip slightly immediately after birth as the baby gets used to new feeding methods and begins to observe its environment — although this is often only a short resting period before growth continues, albeit more steadily.

### The Neonatal Period

Babies are called neonates during the four weeks immediately following birth, then up to one year of age they are known as infants. During this time they are expected to gain 0.85kg (1.87lb) in weight, and to grow more than 2.5cm (1in) per month. Simple calculations suggest that they will often double their initial weight by the time they are six months old, and put on half as much again by their first birthday. This is normally linked with statural changes, which predict that infants will be approximately double their birth height between fourteen and nineteen months, and will attain half their final adult height at about two years of age. A simple calculation can be used to estimate final height on the basis of parental height, to within 10cm (4in) either way. (Note that although this may be an interesting consideration, it is not one on which to place too much reliance.) The child's average weight at this point is approximately four times that at birth. Interestingly it has been noted that if children continued to grow at this amazing rate they would be 3.69m (12ft 3in) tall and weigh several tons at the age of eighteen!

## The First Five Years

Very rapid growth rates persist to a variable point somewhere between the second and third birthday. By now the early years' child has started to grow more slowly than in the first year of life. At two, boys are slightly larger than girls, on average, in both height and weight, but only minimally. Children at this stage are expected to gain between 5 and 7cm (2 and 3in) per year, and to put on between 2.3 and 3.1kg (between 5 and 7lb) in weight. The tendency for growth rate to show steady rather than spectacular gains becomes an increasing factor during this period. By the age of five, children's growth is less noticeable than their change in limb dimension and neural control, which act together to help them function more effectively in their home environment. As this will have a direct bearing on the quality of movement production, it is worthy of comment: thus whilst children may appear gawky and unco-ordinated at times, this is often only a transient factor and one that could be better understood and interpreted.

## Proportional Growth

Essentially the body develops from the top down and from the centre outwards, in that growth, and control, is observed in the head before the shoulders and in the forearms before the hands. The legs and feet are the last to increase in size.

The head is one quarter the size for the overall length at birth, and almost as wide as the shoulders. During the next seven years, the upper body of both boys and girls lengthens and, to a lesser extent, broadens to a point where the head is now only 20 per cent of the overall length and 50 per cent of the total span from shoulder to shoulder.

The increasing breadth of the torso is soon followed by a rapid increase in leg length. At the end of this period there are some signs of a second broadening,

*A range of children from 2 to 5 years old, showing the normal growth pattern.*

which continues at a much slower but consistent rate to the start of puberty.

Increasing height and breadth are triggered by disproportionate growth in key locations of the long levers of the early years' child. Large muscle groups develop first because of the increase in size of the arms and then the legs; specifically this occurs first at the top of the upper arm and the elbow, as well as above and below the knee. The smaller bones, such as those in the wrist, are the last to develop in that they ossify or harden from cartilage more slowly. Conversely the shaft of the long bones such as the femur (thigh) and humerus (upper arm) is already substantially bone at birth.

## Coping with Loss of Performance

This process of change often results in transient, but substantial, loss of simple movement abilities that previously were effectively controlled and confidently performed. Functional deficits are created by covert changes in the system which eventually become obvious but which are nevertheless difficult for some children, and those involved with them, to come to terms with. Some of the more common movement activities which may experience performance losses include grasping, carrying, running, and kicking.

Whilst a reasonable amount is now known about how our abilities are affected during this phase, little advice is given on how best to cope, and what the implications for practice are. This support can be shared by all who work with children so that they receive a common handling which is both positive and considerate.

- Parents could keep a height record and relate it to sitting height, age and relative ability.
- Teachers should focus on the need to make physical activity suited to the developmental age, and should revisit a range of basic skills during periods of most noticeable growth.
- Note the emotional effect on children in your class of having a larger body with less control and without any accompanying increase in self-confidence.
- Let children in on the secret of what to expect when they are growing up. 'When I'm bigger' does not always initially mean 'When I'm better able'.
- Coaches can use questioning and chats to establish how their pupils think they are doing, and to re-emphasize the positive aspects of their performances. Determine how they feel about themselves, to check the reality of their perceptions.

## Motor Development

The increase in physical stature leads the ability to control longer limbs in a purposeful, if slightly more delayed, way. Whilst growth principally occurs at specific points in the large bones, neural control develops in a more continual direction from top to toe. This is by no means an uninterrupted process, as anyone teaching young children how to carry small items of crockery can reliably confirm! This is often because the neural pathway exists in structure before it has sufficient insulation to allow movement messages to be conducted in a single transmission. The message, especially those sent to the extremities of the lower limbs, is delayed at 'roadblocks' where this process, known as 'myelination', has yet to be completed. The net result is jerky and ill-timed movements, though this is often for only a relatively short period of time. It is important to note that these cannot be particularly improved by renewed effort or reward.

- Prepare for children to become less controlled and more frustrated by temporary changes in ability.
- Allow extra individual practice whilst revising key skills with groups of performers.

A small vocabulary of movement experience imposes similar limits on our initial abilities to complete required actions successfully. The well known principle from the currently popular TV quiz series Mastermind — 'I've started so I'll finish' — succinctly explains the difficulty. Deliberate physical movements, under the control of conscious decision-making, are carried out after instructions passed by this immature neural pathway. However, once sent, the code which produces action is virtually unstoppable, regardless of whether the situation still necessitates the same response. Thus it is more likely that unco-ordinated action is a result of movements produced after the event in a situation where the conditions have changed. Children running into each other and boys kicking opponents rather than the ball are examples of running actions that cannot be altered until they have been produced.

- Be patient and understanding with children who produce ill-timed rather than ill-considered movements; it would be as well to suggest that they check again before acting.
- That said, it would appear sensible to provide young children with movement opportunities which are linked to the normal process of proximal to distal (near to far) and encephalocaudal (head to toe). Hand/eye actions should precede foot control and whole body movement.

## Learning Co-ordination

Children learn to co-ordinate some degree of postural control prior to embarking on movement. When they are observed, these movements often tend to emphasize the maintenance of a balanced, upright position prior to the more angled body position required to run, jump and change direction smoothly.

Babies use their greater head and upper arm control to eventually establish superiority over their initially wayward hands. It would appear that they can be motivated to learn by particular manipulation of their environment. The use of mobiles, swings and frames is particularly successful, and keeps their attention for periods in excess of fifteen minutes; these playthings are placed over them at eye level, and to begin with they emphasize the stark contrast between black and white in simple geometrical shapes. After four weeks of regular intervention babies can successfully progress to more complex designs, and thereafter colour patterning.

Once babies can roll onto their stomachs, the process of gaining an upright position develops through support on all limbs, as does leaning, pulling up and standing with assistance. A 'high guard' elevated hand position, a defence reflex anticipating the best support when about to fall, minimal back strength and the co-ordination of reflex actions in the knees and feet are the prerequisites for the onset of walking which occurs anywhere between eight and twenty-one months. Short bouts of practice with targets to grab (padding can prevent accidents when fatigue sets in) provide the opportunity for rapid improvement. Confident walking is the key to opening the door to a much wider range of purposeful activities — but again, these seem to follow a mapped-out pattern, with the child choosing when it is ready to learn.

## The Pattern of Movement Mastery

Initially there is a noticeable difference between the two distinct groups of children within the selected age range. Essentially two- to three- year-olds are still uncertain about their abilities to establish control over their environment, and often embark on play activities with a certain amount of cautious observation prior to direct involvement. When they do initiate individual activity it is often in a modest and undaring way.

The general expectation of two- to three-year olds is that they will commence whole body movements which express different styles of locomotion and conduct them with increasing ease, speed and self-imposed challenge. Walking alone with an erect posture and without the 'high guard' safety mechanism will allow other dependent tasks such as picking up, carrying and replacing objects to be undertaken. Adult observation with appropriate positive reinforcement will make successful repetition an increasingly likely possibility, and will enhance the way children feel about their own growing abilities in the process. This in turn encourages them to attempt new movements for which they have no internal measure of potential success.

## Learning to Walk

When observing walking it has been noted that children initially take short, flat-footed steps with the toes turned outwards; this provides a modicum of assistance at a time when their balance is unpredictable and stepping is rigid and uncomfortable, and when maintaining back posture is difficult for them. However, as a result of more successful practice their arms will be encouraged to drop, and their step length will start to increase as a consequence of higher knee pick-up linked to more active heel-to-toe contact with the ground. Also, making a child practise on surfaces of differing amounts of slope, smoothness and uniformity challenges its ability to cope with its environment, prior to involving additional physical challenges of movement direction or secondary tasks. Although this is considered a central task for life, it appears that its ongoing development does not need to achieve fully matured status before other tasks such as running may be commenced.

## Learning to Run

Running is really quick-contact walking which eventually includes a brief phase of flight in between the support and landing phases, when both feet temporarily lose contact with the ground. Usually it is observed from eighteen months onwards, with most infants running by their second birthday. It is probably the single most important skill to master for future involvement in sports-related activity. Its more involved nature necessitates between two and four years practice to develop reasonable levels of proficiency. This practice, and the associated learning experience, brings observable changes of technical form. Specifically the stride length increases, thus extending the flight phase, and co-ordinated control linked to greater muscular strength allows a more dynamic leg extension at take-off. Synchronized opposite arm and leg swing,

*The young runner in full flight.*

and a generally more cyclical nature of the leg action, may also be noticed, particularly if the movement is recorded and observed with the help of a video camera.

## Jumping

The notion of flight, first evidenced during fledgling running, becomes more fully developed when a child learns to jump. From the same eighteenth-month period, children start to jump down stairs from a one leg take-off to a two-footed landing. At two years they are able to jump on the spot using a simultaneous leg drive and foot extension, and so also learn to bounce; a little later they learn to jump for distance or for maximum height. In fact children learn how to initiate the movement before they have a clear idea of how to control the land-ing. They can jump for distance at three years, and can complete the same jump with object clearance of 35cm (13.7in) by the age of five. Limited arm swing, co-ordinated rocking and full body-lean in the direction of jumping initially reduce take-off speed and thus distance achieved. A bent upper body is often the cause of unbalanced landing with consequent pitching forward onto the knees and then hands. Quicker leg movements and increased abdominal strength allow a more extended landing position, which in turn allows more controlled finish-ing. Jumping for distance is more likely to be successfully accomplished before the leap for height from two feet, which requires a more co-ordinated physical response.

## Hopping

Hopping is the different but related task of taking off and landing on the same leg either for speed or distance. Insufficient leg strength prevents full knee flex-ion and limited single leg balance can effectively cut down the number of repet-itive movements accomplished. Often the preferred foot is the one which is most co-ordinated; it is also the one which is later selected as the dominant foot for kicking. Interestingly it is often the other foot which is the stronger. Children can be expected to hop from 3.5 years, and to complete multiple movements (five or more) within the next five to six months. When linked with stepping, children can then skip (hop-step-hop pattern) or gallop (high step — low step) by 4.5 years and 5.5 years respectively.

Often too much effort initiating the action creates too great a landing force, and loss of control causes the free leg to be grounded prematurely. Short, low movements with low landing forces are best in order to encourage repetition and continuity of technique. Games in which the participants must copy move-ment directions also encourage correct posture and balance. Whilst on this sub-ject, it can be anticipated that girls are likely to hop earlier, better and more con-tinuously than boys of the same age.

## Developing Balance

Having established the importance of balance for single leg movements, it is perhaps timely to consider how this important ability develops. Whilst children can stand still when so inclined, they cannot balance on one leg for long prior to their second birthday, and this ability only marginally improves over the next fourteen months or so. Thus at 3.75 years they progress from walking astride floor lines to walking along them, and to being able to keep heel-to-toe contact. All movements are generally first completed in a forward direction before being attempted backwards, just as straight-line work precedes curved balance walk-ing ability. More adept children alternate the feet, whilst the more timid shuffle across a distance. Low balance beam work can be attempted by the third birth-day. Walking forward on lines, heel to toe, is accomplished a year later, but studies have found that there are still relatively few children who are able to walk ten steps backwards by the age of five.

## Postural Control

Postural control develops before what we might consider full body balance ability, so that children can bend, twist, turn and reach without loss of control; they can also return to an upright position as their reflexes and muscular systems start to mature. These movements often involve manipulation, and generally mature before larger, whole body actions where some body parts move — as in pushing, pulling and running — whilst other parts remain still to enable control. Pushing scooters, sitting on rocking horses, evading someone whilst being chased, and swimming are all useful examples of how this particular type of muscular control can assist movement maturity. Children initially strive to maintain and increase control of their movements before, in a more daring way, they lose this control deliberately in order to experience the pleasure of regaining it. Activity should therefore be organized so that whole body stability and whole body movement permit any such partial and temporary loss of balance. This work could then lead on to faster, dynamic and rotating positional changes. The linking of movement with the balance of different body segments is also a necessary prerequisite for climbing, which utilizes the grip strength present in infancy with arm and leg co-ordination and no small degree of courage.

## Throwing and Catching

Sending, tracking, intercepting and retrieving objects are more sport-related activities that thrill young children and parents alike. Throwing develops from an under-arm lob with differing degrees of release co-ordination, to a mature over-arm form which, as we shall see later, is the foundation for many more complicated sporting movements. Small, light objects which fit small hands and allow tiny fingers to close around them are most suitable initially. First attempts generally demonstrate great force and vigour often not consistent with the size of the movement required. Sometimes this is a matter of mis-judgement, only to be expected on the basis of little prior experience, but more often it is because an inadequate throwing stance is adopted.

Children find that a sideways-on position, with one foot in front of the other, creates greater lower body stability, a bigger distance over which to work against the object, and the possibility of looking and pointing at the intended target. Often the leg on the same side as the throwing arm is placed in advance, which is more useful than facing the target directly, but less co-ordinated than stepping onto the opposite leg. This allows force to be developed by pushing from the back foot as the upper body turns towards the target immediately prior to release. There is little doubt that many children, boys as well as girls, do not appreciate this simple yet important detail, and are thus limited in how able they might eventually become when serving in tennis, smashing in squash or spiking in volleyball. This is possibly not the case abroad where handball and baseball are more evenly popular with both sexes.

*The development of the underarm throw.*

Tracking, intercepting and catching is, ironically, best achieved with a big, moderately heavy and colourful object. This suggests that throwing and catching should be treated as two separate skills and introduced accordingly. Catching is first accomplished with a two-handed, outstretched reach immediately followed by a chest hug to avoid dropping. Small children cannot easily be discouraged from looking at the thrower's face, rather than watching the arc of the object, and timing the reach and hug is also difficult. A beach ball suspended on a string provides the best potential catching opportunity, prior to attaching it to their wrist so that they control the release and do not need to receive a signal from someone else. Rubber balls and bean bags once grasped tend to stay in the palm better than the more tricky tennis balls — and table tennis balls are an even greater challenge. In the same way, quoits should be introduced before hoops.

Once stationary reception has started to improve, short movements to catch slowly moving objects such as parachuted figures can be quickly achieved, after which heavier objects can be made to fall from a greater height out of the space in front of, then slightly above, the child. However, it must be remembered that this type of catching involves making first contact in the close vicinity of the face, and to rush into this progression may test courage more than effort and ability.

Although to a mature adult a throw ought to move an object more quickly than if carrying it on the run, to children both skills will be needed when retrieving objects on the ground. For a child, picking up and carrying whilst running is as important a skill to learn as is drinking fluid whilst running a

*The more complex overarm throw.*

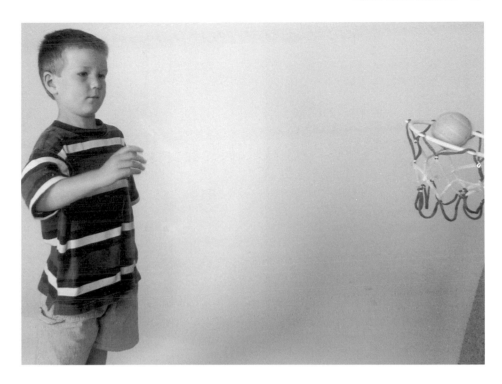

marathon to an adult. It also involves judging how far to run before preparing to throw, and how best to link the two movements. Games on grass over short distances with a recipient who slightly changes position between attempts is a good way of introducing this activity.

## Kicking

Short, clipped movements characterise initial kicking attempts. Inexperienced performers tend to be unable to fully prepare because of fears over losing balance during the preparatory swing. The follow-through is similarly short which creates strong if off-balance ball contacts at ground level. Having the ball placed on the ground, rather than complicating it with an upward throw, and placing the non-striking leg alongside the ball in the required direction, can help improve the quality of performance.

In essence, the early years' child rapidly gains control over its limbs, and should be encouraged to work on bodily control in early practice. As these children grow and gain in strength, control and co-ordination, the manipulation of objects and more advanced forms of movement become appropriate. The key is to watch for their interest, and then to provide opportunities in which their level of physical readiness suggests that they have a high chance of success.

*Kicking with an aid to control.*

# CHAPTER TWO

# Do First, Think Later

Children under the age of seven are primarily physical beings in that they make sense of their world through their physical interactions with it. This is clearly apparent in very young children which develop their thinking or cognitive abilities by first doing. For example, an understanding of hot and cold is achieved through the physical sensations that are felt when a child touches something hot or cold: the association with the word and its meaning and the physical sensation is then established. Moreover it is only through the physical experience that this level of understanding can be achieved. There are many other examples where a clear link exists between a child's physical experience and its cognitive development — yet when children are placed in the environment that is supposed to develop their cognitive functioning, namely school, this link seems to be forgotten. Clearly sport has a role to play in this process, yet in schools very little time is given to physical activity, and often the first thing that is cancelled when there are other more 'important' things to do is the PE lesson.

So it appears that the current conviction regarding childhood development is that physical activity develops the body, but not the mind. Thus when new parents enrol their children at school they are encouraged to read, draw and write with them, but rarely do teachers encourage them to share any other physical activity with them as a means to stimulate and enhance their cognitive capabilities. This is a mistake, and educators both within and outside sport need to re-evaluate their teaching premise, to the effect that coaching and teaching young children physical activities can be the cornerstone not only for their physical development, but also for their cognitive development. Thus a child who engages in meaningful physical activity can develop a more useful understanding of many things, such as decision making, perceptual awareness, improved memory functioning and creativity, to name but a few.

We still operate in a culture that tends to separate mind and body, and it is essential that this common perception is reversed so we recognize that working with the body is by definition working with the mind, that the two operate in harmony. In fact the possibilities for working through the body to enhance cognitive functioning are endless; they have just not been fully explored. The main aim of this chapter is to examine ways in which both coaches working within sport and teachers working within PE can strengthen the links between the physical and cognitive development of young children by enhancing their participation in physical activity, and allowing them to let 'their bodies do the talk-ing'. In order to do this we must first have a good understanding of cognitive development.

## The Psychology of Child Development

There are a number of critical theories on child development, but we will focus on just two: Piaget's theory of cognitive development, and Erikson's theory of psycho-social development. Both these theories go far beyond the specific age range for this chapter, however it is important to briefly examine them in their entirety.

### *Piaget's Theory of Cognitive Development*

The work of Piaget in the sixties has had a huge influence on the understanding of intellectual growth that occurs from infancy to adulthood; also the way in which schools currently teach children has been considerably affected by his theories. The main emphasis of his work is that cognitive development involves definitive qualitative changes, and that as a result there are critical differences between adults and children in the way in which they think. For the first time he presented the notion that cognitive development, much like physical development, goes through identifiable stages, each of which can be related to particular developing cognitive skills and to approximate chronological ages. For the purpose of this chapter we shall briefly explain the characteristics of each stage in order to understand more fully the concept of cognitive development.

**The Sensory Motor Stage, 0—2 years**
When a baby enters this world it does so with a few basic body movements that are necessary for survival. These are developed into a sophisticated movement repertoire referred to as 'schemas', and it is through these schemas that babies make sense of the world and all the physical, psychological and emotional experiences that they encounter. These schemas build up into very complex movement patterns and, given the lack of formal speech capabilities, are a powerful form of communication.

**The Pre-Operational Stage, 2—4 years**
The two-year-old has now developed considerably and is able to operate from a very different perspective. He or she now enjoys considerable internal representation of thought and ideas, largely as a result of interaction with the world and an innate predisposition to explore.

**The Concrete Operational Stage, 7—12 years**
At this stage the child now becomes capable of logical thought. The hallmark of

*A child develops his motor schema.*

this stage as identified by Piaget is that the children achieve 'conservation concepts': in lay-person terms this means that they can begin to order the world around them through numbers, mass and weight. They can also begin to understand relational terms (A is longer than B).

**The Formal Operational Stage, 12 years and up**
Children can now start to think in abstract terms, they can follow reasoned arguments, and can develop and test their own hypotheses. They can think in terms of hypothetical situations — the future — by combining memory and experience to solve ideological problems.

The stages of development as described by Piaget emphasize the internal mental activity that children engage in as a direct result of their universal tendency to explore their environment. Children will build models of it, and will reflect on the adequacy of these models. Whilst more recent research has pointed out that all children may not pass through these developmental stages in the same way, there are still considerable similarities that may be observed between children, and Piaget's work still provides us with a valuable framework from which to understand the process of cognitive development. Thus as coaches, we should be providing abundant opportunities for children to explore and reflect, and we should be looking for ways in which we might adopt a guided discovery approach to coaching, rather than using methods that rely solely on explicit instruction.

When coaching very young children it is crucial that we are aware of their cognitive stage of development and construct practices that are appropriate. For example, when teaching very young children a basic jumping skill it would be beneficial to let them explore the concept of 'jumping' by allowing them to try it out in a number of different ways. By doing this they can begin to understand the feeling of jumping, and this will be more beneficial than just giving an explanation of how to do it.

## Erik Erikson's Theory of Psycho-Social Development

The work of Erik Erikson on psycho-social development is also useful to examine, as he proposes a model that maps the development and growth of an individual into the complete 'self'. In a similar way to Piaget he presents a stage approach to development that he has described as the 'ages of man'. We will briefly consider some of these stages.

### Trust, 0—2 years
The child is learning about his physical and emotional environment, and who the important people are within it. It is at this stage that children like to develop familiar routines, as this brings them greater reassurance and certainty.

### Autonomy, 2—4 years
During this stage the child begins to recognize the existence of free will. Children develop the ability to choose what they want to do, and will enjoy experimenting with how to put this into action.

### Imitation, 4—6 years
Children will be reproducing the world that they know around them; hence games often imitate everyday events such as going shopping or playing schools. Clearly the role models that children have to imitate will have a significant effect on their development.

### Competence, 6—12 years
This stage reflects children's need to be able to 'do' things in order to be accepted by their peers. A great deal of social evaluation takes place during these years.

### Identity, 12—18 years
The critical development from childhood to adult: the main characteristic of this stage is the search for the answer to the question 'Who am I?'

Whilst the relevance of such developmental psychological theories might not be immediately apparent, they are useful in enhancing our understanding of child development. This is something that the majority of coaching courses do not even mention, even though a high proportion of coaches will work with young children. They can also be used as a way of checking that our coaching has indeed taken these developmental stages on board, and that it reflects them in an appropriate way.

## How Do Children Learn?

In order for coaches to be effective when working with children there needs to be some understanding of the mechanisms by which children learn. Essentially learning must be viewed as an active rather than as a passive process, one in which there is an interaction between the learner and the teacher, and the environment. However, it is also clear that there are fundamental differences between adults and children in the way in which learning takes place, particularly when the child is viewed from the developmental perspective, as previously mentioned.

### The Early Years

During the early years of a child's life learning occurs at a rapid rate, with the child soaking up information at every opportunity, as a sponge might soak up water. Take the instance of a child being translocated to a foreign country: he or she may not receive any formal 'teaching' of the indigenous language, but nevertheless he is able to 'absorb' it as it is spoken around him, and will demonstrate its subtle nuances with remarkable accuracy from a very early age. So it seems as if language is learnt without effort.

When attempting to develop sports skills in young children, the area of concern is motor learning. This has been defined as 'A relatively permanent change in the performance of a motor skill resulting from practice or past experience' (Kerr, 1982). What should concern us is how this process can be enhanced or achieved most effectively.

## The Interpretation of Intelligence

As humans we have a highly developed brain that allows us to effectively process large amounts of information — more than that, we have the ability to generate ideas and then to store them. These processes all contribute to what psychologists refer to as intelligence. Sadly this term has often been misrepresented, and as a result, interpretations of intelligence are just as often misleading. Intelligence takes many different forms, and certainly should not be thought of as simply the ability to do IQ tests: these only assess verbal and mathematical concepts, and as such are rather limiting as a means of determining human intelligence.

The model by Robert Fisher (1992) helps to illustrate this point:

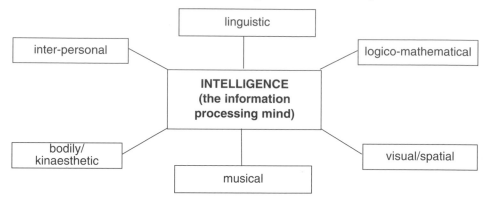

If this view is adopted then we will have a broader view of human functioning, and will recognize that the ability to be effective in sport requires intelligence. It is usually very apparent to a coach that some children's bodily or kinaesthetic intelligence is more advanced than that of others — sometimes this is referred to as 'talent', or being 'gifted'. Moreover it is an important part of human functioning that can be developed.

## Developing Talent

Let us consider in more detail the mechanisms that we use to develop this information-processing ability (in Robert Fisher, 1992, adapted from Sternberg 1984):

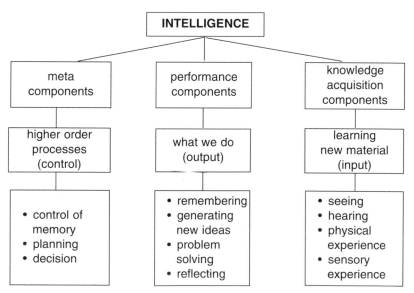

In the above model there are three main components that are involved in our ability to process information: the metacomponents, the performance components, and the knowledge acquisition components. The key factor to this model is that all the underlying processes and components can be developed and enhanced  through effective learning strategies. The view taken by some psychologists is that we should concern ourselves with teaching our children to think, and in this way we can develop the many different forms of human intelligence. Clearly the teaching of physical skills therefore has a significant role to play in all of this — perhaps one that has been overlooked in the narrow, two-dimensional view of intelligence that has predominated in Western culture.

If we explore the concept of bodily or kinaesthetic intelligence in more depth, there are a number of discrete skills that are associated with it, all of which have a significant role to play in the development of young athletes. These are skills of:

| | |
|---|---|
| manipulation | e.g. holding |
| construction | e.g. arranging |
| projection | e.g. throwing, kicking, catching |
| agility | e.g. running, jumping, balancing |
| communication | e.g. gesture, non-verbal communication. |

(R.Fisher, 1992)

*A child explores his skills of manipulation.*

## *Schmidt's Schema Theory*

These psycho-motor skills all require mental processing: there really is no such thing as a purely physical skill. The way in which these skills are acquired has been under scrutiny for a number of years, and a number of significant theories have been put forward to explain the process. Perhaps the most important of these is the Schema theory that was proposed by Schmidt in 1975, which allows us to understand how we develop and perfect movement patterns. Below is a diagrammatic adaptation of the model:

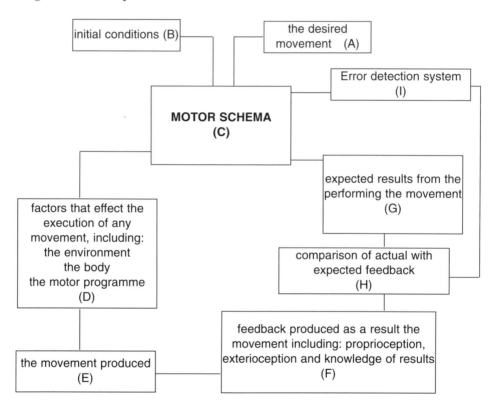

This model may at first appear to be rather complicated, but if we consider the following example of a pass in football, it will become clearer.  The desired outcome is (A), and this movement must be executed in a moment of time that is our starting point, (B): for the purposes of our example it will be in the last ten minutes of a cup final. The motor schema that has to be activated is one of kicking, (C). However, unless we consider the factors that are going to affect the kicking schema, the action will not be successful. The specifics of the motor program are the part of the body involved, and the environmental conditions, (D). In our example the motor program for striking the ball is with the inside of the foot; the body part will be the right foot, and the environmental conditions are of a wet muddy pitch. As a consequence,  there will need to be more power put into the kick if it is to be successful. The length of the pass is approximately ten metres, to the player running into position. The movement is then executed, (E). Following the movement there will be immediate feedback from a number of sources, starting with the body. This is referred to as proprioception, secondly the environment is exterioception, and last is the outcome of the movement, (F).

The feedback generated from our example was as follows: proprioception revealed that the wrong part of the foot made contact with the ball, and exterioception indicated that the player for whom the pass was intended made his run longer than the length of the pass. There is a comparison made between (F) what actually happened, and (H) what was expected to happen. This comparison (G) forms the basis of an error detection system (I). The result of this analysis is then stored, and can be used again as part of a now slightly modified motor schema.

The main premise of Schimdt's theory is that in order for us to develop effective motor schemas, we should expose the children to a large variety of different conditions. It is through using motor movements under a variety of conditions that we can develop and enhance the motor schema: the more highly developed the motor schema, the better the skills of the children.

So what does this mean in coaching? The essential message is that you should spend time practising skills under conditions which are as varied as possible. If we use this passing example, the coaching message is clear — namely, ensure your drills are varied — using both feet, using long and short passes, and using it with defenders or as an isolated skill. The bigger the exposure that you give the children of 'the pass', the more adapted and the more effective their motor schema. Clearly it is crucial to adopt this approach with young children, because this is the stage when major physical developments take place. So perhaps the message is to allow for a variety of movement patterns, rather than concentrating on fine tuning and developing just a few. In the long run you will serve your athlete better.

## Physical Activity and Imagination

Young children live in a magical world, and as coaches we need to rediscover the child's-eye view, and understand that it is fundamentally different from our own: if we take this perspective we can better understand a child's imagination and its creative powers.

Imagination allows us to transcend the present and to engage in fantasies, visions and plans, and to summon up solutions to problems. Within sport there are many possibilities when a child might use its imagination to enhance its performance. Often in sport we assume that we are in the business of 'telling' young children what they should be doing; instead, however, we need to be looking for ways in which they can develop their imagination through the physical activity. If we do not give children this opportunity we can limit their horizon, and so also limit the possibilities whence we might learn from them.

*A child develops her climbing schema.*

*A coach and child having a fun time on the trampoline.*

We often hold on to the view that the child's view is somehow inferior to our own. However, by moving away from this fixed position, learning becomes a two-way process, with each becoming the wiser.

## The Coach's Working Practice

So, having recognized the benefit of encouraging young children to use their imagination when they are engaged in physical activities, how can the coach of young children do this? What would need to change in his current working practices to embrace this?

One way in which adults can gain an insight into the child's world is through listening. This may sound very basic, but how often do we listen to their conversations or explanations of events? If we took time to do this we would be better able to tune into their perceptions and imaginations. We can also try to join their world through stories, images and play. You may be thinking that this has little application to sport and to the development of physical skills. However, if we just question the way we have done things in the past, we can develop creative and innovative techniques in coaching, especially with very young children. Consider these possible simple applications:

Say in tennis you are working on developing power: ask the child to imagine that the ball is made of fire, so he or she must hit it as far away as possible.

Say in gymnastics you are working on jumping skills to encourage the children to jump as far as possible: mark out a river and introduce the idea that there are crocodiles in the water — then suggest to the children that they must jump as far as possible to ensure that they are not eaten up!

As a warm-up routine, choose games which use such ploys as pirates or even sticky toffee: this gives the children the opportunity to develop a story through which running and basic skills can be introduced.

By introducing such simple imaginative methods in your coaching sessions not only can you develop imagination through physical activity, but you can also increase the children's enjoyment of your sessions. Extensive research has indicated that children take part in sport largely seeking enjoyment and to have fun. Surely it is therefore prudent to look at ways in which coaches can provide this.

## Understanding Creativity

Allowing children to use their imagination when they are engaged in physical activity is the starting point to developing creative athletes. One only has to think of some of the truly great athletes to realize that they were very creative people, and and that they brought this creativity to their sporting endeavours. But what is creativity? Psychologists have generally classified it as having the following three components:

*Fluency*, or the number of ideas that an individual can come up with.
*Flexibility*, or an individual's ability to adapt to new circumstances or new challenges.
*Originality*, or the extent to which ideas are fresh and novel.

Highly creative people tend to be well endowed with all three of these attributes. Let us consider some examples that illustrate the above. Firstly, Dick Fosbury of Fosbury flop fame: before he dreamed up his innovative technique, athletes straddled the bar and their method was a limiting factor in the height they were able to achieve. Fosbury's new technique was highly original, bringing him gold in the 1968 Olympic Games, and radically changing the face of high jump forever.

Artistic gymnastics is a sport that is always looking for the innovative, and traditionally any new technique is named after the gymnast who first performs it in competition; an example of this would be the Korbut flick. The first time this movement was performed on beam was in 1972 — up until this point no one had ever done any acrobatic elements on the beam: now eight-year-olds accomplish it with ease. Another gymnastic element that dramatically changed the sport was the Yurchenko vault. This was first performed by Natalia Yurchenko in 1984 and involved a round-off take-off from the board, rather than the normal run-up. When she first performed it the judges did not know how to score it, and initially gave it 0 as a void vault. However, after much discussion it was allowed, and it is now routinely performed.

Again, both these examples demonstrate a flexible and original approach in their conception and execution.

Creative athletes make sport exciting to watch and to be a part of. Just consider the ice-dancers Torvill and Dean: in the eighties they transformed the world of ice-dancing by demonstrating exceptional fluency, flexibility and originality in their performances; for their Bolero routine they were rewarded with a complete sweep of 6s.

## Developing Creative Potential

We might ask what this has got to do with coaching small children. Speaking as a coach, what is being done in our sessions to help develop the creative potential in our athletes is probably very little, but there are ways in which we can remedy the situation.

Firstly, we might help to develop fluency through allowing the free flow of ideas. This is often refered to as 'brainstorming', but this interpretation is not really relevant to sport because in order for the process to be effective, it must be non-judgmental: you must be careful not to reject anything the children offer, the aim being to allow them to develop independent thought and creativity through physical activity.

Secondly, we can help develop flexibility by avoiding one-track thinking: allow children to come up with different solutions to a problem, ask them to think about it from a number of angles, let them experiment with different ideas. Move away from the idea that there is only one right way to do something — clearly this is not the case otherwise the likes of Pele would have no place in sport.

Thirdly, we can often help develop originality in children by allowing them to recognize that many of their ideas are original for them. This generates an excitement in the child that will encourage it to explore variation; it will also help to establish self-confidence, and create a coaching environment where individuality is respected. Who knows — you might be seeing the next Dick Fosbury take shape!

## Social Development Through Sport

Sport can have a significant role to play in the social development of any child. It is often through early participation in sport that children make significant and possibly long-lasting friendships; this is one good reason why taking part in any sport should be viewed as a pleasant social activity as well as a means to stay in shape. Moreover, fostering this perspective is clearly worthwhile as it is more likely to ensure a life-long involvement in sport.

However, the coach needs to be aware of the psycho-social development of the children he teaches in order to create an environment within which they can flourish.

Very young children will often still be primarily tied to one main caretaker, and when they enter your class it might be their first encounter with a large group of children; it might also be their first experience of carrying out an activity in the absence of their carer — so all things considered, this particular transition might be quite a daunting prospect for all concerned. Some children will make it with ease, whilst others will need time to adjust to their new environment.

Within a group of three- to four-year-olds there can be a lot of variation in the amount of social interaction that they have experienced; for instance, some children may already be in full-time school, whilst others may still be spending most of their time at home. Therefore it is very important that you establish what their previous experiences have been, because this will enable you to have a better understanding of the children with whom you are working.

Another aspect that needs to be considered is the view that small children have of the world, how it colours their perceptions and influences the types of activity they can handle.

You will find that it is primarily an egocentric one. For instance, young children will find great difficulty in taking part in activities that require a lot of co-operation; thus it would be inappropriate to expect twenty-two four-year-olds to play a game of football with any degree of success, for several reasons: first, small children will find it physically very difficult to pass the ball; second, they want to be doing it for themselves; and third, the fact that another child might be wanting the ball is really of very little concern to them. Developing skills in the first instance will therefore be more effective if the coach works on an individual basis.

Taking part in any sporting activity can develop the ability of young children to co-operate with each other, helping to foster feelings of trust and mutual respect, both valuable social lessons to learn. Sport also brings together people from a wide range of social and ethnic backgrounds, and provides the opportunity for constructive integration. However, as a coach you must be sure that you are capable of creating this type of positive atmosphere: it is therefore essential that you leave any personal prejudices or stereotypes at home. Furthermore, remember that racial and sexual discrimination is illegal.

## Practical Hints for Coaches

Do develop a sound knowledge of child development, and look for ways to put theory into practice in your sessions.
Do evaluate your current coaching practices.
Do be receptive to the children's ideas.
Do develop a good knowledge of the children in your group.
Do talk to them.

## Practical Hints for Parents

Do talk to the coach.
Do watch your child participate.
Do encourage your child to become a physical being.
Do get feedback from your child.
Do check for enjoyment levels.

CHAPTER THREE

# The Good, The Bad and The Indifferenet

## Home-Based Activity

Parents are in an ideal position to provide early, stimulating movement opportunities for their children. The selection of appropriate activities which are both challenging and progressive can start at home long before there is a need to involve others.

*A child and parent enjoy target practice.*

All the studies carried out in the early part of this century suggest that regular play opportunities, with familiar observers and encouragers in attendance, are essential to the learning process of babies and very young children. This is accomplished through the physical manipulation of their environment. Once objects have been discovered, they absorb the child's attention until such time as their developmental value becomes exhausted. It is just before this point that parental provision of slightly more advanced equipment ensures that the desire to play (children consider it work) maintains interest in the learning process. Thus creating and maintaining that learning environment, as well as spending sufficient time as the supportive audience, is a fundamental parental function. Some activities appropriate to this age are as follows:

• A child sees and hears before it can consistently touch, grasp and manipulate. To start with it is therefore best to introduce a variety of clear, repeatable noises which mimic domestic sounds, and simple patterns which emphasize contrast in colour.

• An effective ploy is to suspend various soft objects with human faces just within the child's reach; they should be close enough for the child to see and mouth them, and to attempt initial grasping movements. Once upper forearm control is perceived, the height at which the individual objects are strung up can be varied so the child will learn the relationship between distance and reach.

• Soft flooring and enough space to allow choice of direction can encourage the child to roll about and crawl; be careful to remove furniture which has sharp edges. Placing familiar objects in sight but out of reach can motivate children to explore. Sometimes other, slightly older children can be equally motivating; however, they may also provide a form of entertainment which encourages watching rather than doing.

• A footstool, a firm beanbag, a child's chair and the back of a sofa all provide just the right purchase to help children gain an upright position for the first time.

• Clear floors and encouraging adults can then trigger fledgling steps. This is the basis for most of the simple movement skills previously outlined.

• Once walking and running have been mastered, children will want to experiment with related movement patterns. Pushing toy cars and riding scooters help the cyclical leg action later used in running, stepping and hopping. Bouncing activities, on mattresses placed on the floor, can encourage bodily control in the air, co-ordination and jumping ability.

• Tricycles, cars and bicycles with stabilizers soon follow. They allow continued pushing opportunities in more co-ordinated movements which build on the cyclical stepping reflexes present in young children soon after birth. Steering skills improve hand/eye linkage and decision-making, and sitting on a saddle leads to postural training for back and abdominal muscles.

## Facility-Based Activity

In **local parks or grassed areas,** children can run for the sheer exhilaration of the activity.

•   They will often incorporate skipping, as well as swinging movements if the parents are in attendance.

•   Various challenges can be set, using the geography of the area: weaving in and out of trees, which starts to develop agility skills; running on lines for co-ordination; and balancing on edging, wooden planks, stepping stones and short posts for overall body control.

•   Encourage children to run towards a designated object or landmark: this practises the idea of covering the shortest distance whilst at the same time it provides a foundation for upright movement posture. Emphasizing a certain goal, such as a tree or a bench, reduces the tendency to notice the effort involved and thus starts to develop whole body fitness.

•   Walking on low walls is another popular pursuit with children, partly because they can walk side by side with their parents, and because they are at the same height. Further challenge can be provided a) by learning to walk with the feet pointing along the brickwork rather than having them splayed out, and b) by making controlled turns.

•   Sturdy, smooth fencing with horizontal links provides more than one climbing opportunity, not just to get off the ground, but also to transfer the weight across spaces. See how far the child can go without touching the grass underneath: this starts to develop the important climbing skill of using hands and feet in a co-ordinated way.

**Playgrounds**  have improved so much in recent years that they are a must for enhancing early body control:

•   They provide essential opportunities for children to develop upper body strength and co-ordination through activities such as swinging and climbing, also holding on to, lowering themselves from, and crossing from one piece of equipment to another.

• They can encourage co-operation and a knowledge of safe practice, and they can help children to overcome their fears; for instance, using equipment which involves a substantial climb presents a major challenge to the initially timid. Using steep or spiralling slides can develop great self-confidence, and can fuel interactions with other children and parents for many hours.

• Spinning rides can help children develop their judgement of speed, and using a swing teaches them control of speed and range of movement. Taking turns and co-operating with playmates and adults are also tested out in such places.

• Rubberized or bark flooring, together with better training-shoe technology, allows a much wider range of activity than was previously safe.

*Comparison of protection from different shoe types.*

**Indoor play areas**  now enjoy the advantages of increased height, improved sound effects and little queuing; they therefore increase even further the opportunities for stimulating play and at the same time assuring fitness development. It is important to children that their parents watch and encourage them ('Dad, put that paper down!') and to a lesser extent exercise some control; they are also needed to provide refreshments on an ongoing basis at such centres.

• Encourage children to use activities where the muscles of the upper body and stomach are emphasized.

• Try to ensure that children use the different areas and the variety of equipment equally, and do not concentrate their efforts on just one sort. Using all the levels and all the equipment provides greater scope for self-development.

• Parents should visit the play area earlier in the morning or at other quiet times so that they can be actively involved without preventing other children.

With the advent of theme pools — these often with an inviting tropical environment — **water-based activities** are now of similar diversity and scope.

Furthermore, many pools have a gently sloping walkway into the shallow end, so that not being able to manage the metal steps is not the barrier it used to be. Once in, the main priority is being confident in water so that movement towards the interesting range of play equipment on offer becomes possible. Aquatic skills for young children include:

•   Standing with support prior to standing alone; learning how to lose, and then regain an upright position a) whilst wearing a buoyancy aid, and b) when being held by the hand; being splashed; and walking and holding onto the side rail.

•   Bouncing, jumping on the spot, hopping in the water, kicking and pulling cupped hands through the water are all useful activities, and often linked to simple games and nursery rhymes.

•   Gently pulling children on their front, back and side allows them to experience the thrill of movement before they are able to produce or control such movement themselves.

•   Running through shallow water on the beach or as allowed in some swimming pools gives the same sense of moving quickly whilst providing opportunities for imaginative play.

•   The next challenges might include climbing on animals or low islands with fountains, playing underneath watersprays, and shooting down short, traditional water slides; children still in arm bands can safely enjoy all these provided their parents are close by to keep an eye on them.

**Playing with soft rubber balls** provides further opportunity to develop a wide range of skills, although play activities need to be controlled in order to be really beneficial; here are some principles for effective practice:

•   Collect or retrieve first, throwing second. If parents send the objects, then the children will gain confidence in their own movement abilities before throwing is as well developed.

•   Consider throwing objects which allow more time in which to retrieve. Parachuted soldiers, soft frisbees, disc aerobies and HKT balls travel more slowly and therefore give increased movement potential; this is important to the child when it is tracking, prior to receiving.

•   Introduce holding and bouncing separately prior to combining them in order to catch.

•   Throw small, heavier objects to large targets: this requires judgement and develops accuracy. Throwing for distance can wait until upper arm strength and technique improve.

•   Use soft, largish objects for catching because these have a greater chance of staying in the hand. Cloth-covered balls, bean bags and light juggling balls are of such a texture as to aid grip; moreover they are often brightly coloured, which helps tracking.

## A Word About Equipment

The next step would be to progress from introducing skills with general equipment to using sport-specific material. Most activities have developed ranges of equipment which have been adapted and modified to suit the proportions of young children.

*A range of equipment adapted for young children.*

•   When purchasing a football, netball or basketball select a smaller size 2 or 3, rather than an adult size 5.

•   Consider the colour so that it can be watched for direction and spin. A return cord may also be useful.

•   When selecting a baseball or a rounders bat, choose one of shorter than normal length, and one which has a protective grip, because this encourages children to hold it in the correct way. A large plastic tee on which to place the equally large ball reduces the difficulty of learning to strike.

- Using a short-handled tennis racket where most of the shaft is removed similarly improves control. This adaptation reduces the weight of the implement at a time when children do not have the strength or the endurance to carry a full-size racket properly. Not using a modified version will eventually cause poor gripping and cut down the length of rallies.

- Also helpful to children are hoops, goals and nets that can be adjusted up and down. Starting with a low goal or net encourages success, and the height can be raised gradually to increase challenge. These adjustable goals are commercially available for budding netball and basketball shooters.

- It is more appropriate to use mini sport pitches or court dimensions together with modified, child-friendly rules when playing with young children. Bounces and more touches of the ball would also need to be allowed in conjunction with a low net in mini volleyball, for example.

There is no doubt that children benefit from activity, even if it often remains self-selected. Organised input can ensure that a wider range of experiences is introduced, and these are more likely to suit a child's current abilities whilst retaining the level of challenge. This fosters the 'learning how to learn' premise, and is a better basis for the genetic school-based activity programme they will experience during the primary years. So what do we look for in a well constructed programme, particularly for those operating in the non-school sector?

## The Structure of Classes

There are many different ways in which a sport class that is operating outside school can be organized. The purpose of this section is to try and identify the key issues regarding structure in order that a child gains maximum benefit from taking part.

### *The Coach*

First of all find out who is taking the class: you need to know exactly what their qualifications are, and when they qualified. Someone whose qualification dates from twenty years back may be out of date, and possibly not in the best position to teach your child. Every governing body of sport will have a recognized qualification system which coaches must take in order to practise. A coach may also have attended courses put on by the National Coaching Foundation. These are a valuable addition to most governing body awards, and show that the coach has attended courses covering child-related issues as well.

You also need to ask if the coach has been police checked: if he has not, we strongly recommend that you do not enrol your child with this coach. Some local authorities automatically run these checks on any coach they employ, but do not assume that this has been done. Unfortunately it is now coming to light just how easy it is for paedophiles to work within sport, simply as a result of inconsistent application. You have a right to this information as you are putting your child into someone else's hands, and you need to have confidence in them. If you are unhappy with any of the responses to your questions, we repeat: do not enrol your child.

## The Time of Classes

When a class takes place is important with regard to a child. Clearly this will in the first instance depend on whether the child attends school or nursery, or if they are younger than this. Let us first consider children of pre-school age, and for these we must find out if the timing of the class fits in with the child's normal routine. If a child normally has a nap in the afternoon, then it would be unwise to enrol him or her in a class that runs during what would be sleep time. Classes that are held in the morning often suit the activity levels of pre-school children much better, and as a result they will get much more out of it; it is not really appropriate to expect very young children to 'pay attention' if they are tired.

The same basic rule applies to children who are attending school, and in particular, after-school sport activities need to be put into the overall context of the child's life. Children vary greatly in their ability to cope with the demands of school, and for some the end of the day is simply not a good time. In this case it might therefore be unrealistic to expect them to participate fully in a sports class if they are not in the mood to do so. If this is the case then there are many classes which operate at a weekend, and which might be more appropriate to begin with.

The above may sound very obvious, but in reality parents and carers often have the notion that they want the child to follow a particular sport, and when they find somewhere that is offering that sport, they enrol the child in the class without any further consideration, rather than really examining its needs at that moment in time. A great deal of pressure is put on parents and carers nowadays to ensure that their children are 'doing the right thing', regardless of the needs of the child. This in turn can put a lot of stress on the child, who might simply be too tired to participate fully, but who may be viewed by the coach as being uncooperative.

## The Location of Classes

Equally important is where the classes are to be held. There are many different environments in which a sport can take place, and it is crucial that the facility is safe, and that it is appropriate for the activity in which the children are involved. For example, a swimming lesson that is to take place in a cold pool is not appropriate for very young children; nor is a football class where children are expected to use a full-size pitch.

## Further Key Issues

There are other questions which you should ask before enrolling your child on any sports course; these include:

### The Ratio of Coaches to Children

This will depend on the type of activity that the child is taking part in. But in order for your child to have any valuable experience from participating, the coach needs to be doing more than just 'crowd control'. Where the activity involves more safety concerns — for example in gymnastics, swimming and climbing, to name but a few — the ratio needs to be considerably smaller.

### The Length of the Class

A child's ability to be actively engaged in one particular activity when it is very young is limited because its concentration span is short. Look for classes of between half and three-quarters of an hour for very young children; this can increase as the child matures and its interest in the activity develops.

The number of times a week that a class takes place is also important. In some sports there exists a great urgency to involve very young children in multiple training sessions per week at a very young age; this is especially true if the coach deems that the child has a 'talent' for the sport. However, be aware that by specializing too young the child may become too narrowly focused and will assuredly miss out on other interesting activities. Nevertheless, if the child is enjoying the activity and wants to participate more frequently, then this would be appropriate.

Choosing the right activity, at the right time of day and in a welcoming environment, is very important. This is the child's first experience of sport, and of those people directly involved with it, so taking care to ensure it is both pleasurable and rewarding is well worth the effort.

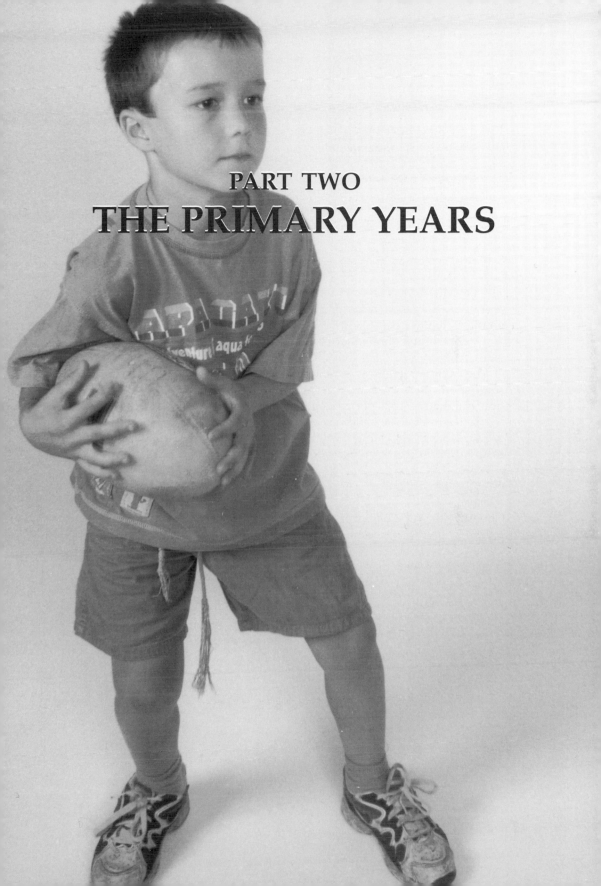

PART TWO
# THE PRIMARY YEARS

*As children progress into the primary years there is a shift in emphasis with regard to the key issues. Recognition that these skill-hungry years provide essential opportunities for children between seven and eleven years of age to pick up a wide array of general sports skill in preparation for later, more specialized involvement will be addressed.*

*The issue of skill development is considered from a number of different perspectives including co-ordination, maturation and milestones in movement.*

*At this stage understanding why children participate in sport and the psychological benefits that can be acquired from doing so are considered.*

*Finally, this section considers key areas to do with identification and nurturing of talent through effective coaching methodologies.*

# CHAPTER FOUR

# The Skill-Hungry Years

In the child aged between seven and eleven the co-ordinated functioning of its developing system can now demonstrate real and purposeful control over the environment in ways too many and varied to list. The early years child has undergone accelerated growth and developmental changes at rates which suggest they cannot be sustained for long. It is, therefore, not surprising that whilst structural change is still a consistent theme during this middle developmental period, consolidation and steadier progress are more to the fore. What, then, are the physical expectations of this period, and how may a knowledge of developmental events help guardians in ensuring a happy, positive foundation for life and sport?

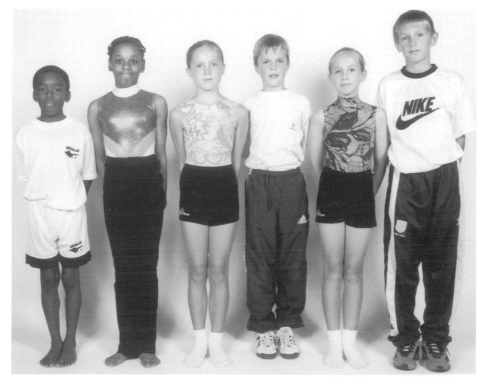

*Who is the oldest? See end of chapter 10.*

## Size and Weight

The rate of structural growth slows considerably during this period as if in anticipation of the maelstrom of puberty which follows. This trend reflects the noticeably uneven rate of growth throughout childhood, and whilst change in size can still be measured, it is not as dominant a feature as in either of the phases which precede or follow it.

### Height

Boys develop slowly as regards average height, from 125cm (4ft 1in) at age seven to 145cm (4ft 9in) four years later. Girls lag only marginally behind boys in terms of overall height until the age of nine when, for the next two years at least, they can be as tall if not taller than their counterparts. This can be partially attributed to the basic premise that girls are a few weeks further ahead in their maturational development from early in the pregnancy, and they maintain that advantage in a number of ways until they commence their adolescent growth spurt, a considerable time before boys. Initially this can be seen in terms of their greater desire to attempt new tasks and the finer degree of control they can bring to their efforts. And whilst boys start to catch up on functional ability, girls' growth rate inches ahead to the point where, for the only time in life, their size and strength allow them to perform at least as well, if not better than boys.

The obvious suggestion is that not only should equal opportunity to activity be a feature throughout the middle years, but that girls ought to be given more opportunities to try new activities and to learn new skills before boys. Their motivational level and the expectancy that they will be initially more successful make this a worthwhile course of action. This is especially the case where control and technique are important parameters. It also suggests that, if anything, activities conducted in mixed settings are more likely to elevate the performance of girls and have a less positive effect on boys at the same time. These are obviously sensitive issues that could allow positive discrimination at a time when girls are better physically placed to accept and gain from advanced activities.

### Weight Change

The story of weight change throughout this period is similar, with 'filling out' and 'becoming heavier to lift' observations being reflected in a steady increase in measured weight. Boys and girls gain on average 16kg (35lb) during the four years between their seventh and eleventh birthdays, with little real advantage to either sex. As seems reasonable, the slightly greater average height of girls at age nine corresponds with a marginally greater average weight from thereafter. This suggests a real difference from the early years, where children's growth merely leads to a redistribution of their weight rather than sizeable weight gains per se.

As this means that children will, on average, weigh 39kg (86lb) by the age of eleven, the significant change in bulk may be worth measuring at regular intervals, namely those which correspond with height changes. This weight gain reflects the fact that, at this age, children use up to 10 per cent of their energy intake for growth alone. This compares with figures of 40 per cent of energy intake for growth in infancy, and 20 per cent during early childhood. This decelerated trend is interesting in that relatively more energy can, and should be, expended on physical activity. Recording height, weight, food intake and exercise type becomes, from this age, worthy of analysis as a result of simple comparison. Failure to maintain a sensible calorific balance now can be identified as the origin of much anguish later in life, when control and remediation are much more difficult to effect.

## Coaching Tips

•   Make the most of girls' maturity advantage by introducing them to activities which require balance, turning and well co-ordinated movements first. Give boys more practice at activities which require greater control first, and avoid progressing too quickly.

•   Keep records of height, weight, activity levels and food intake. Do periods of intense play, skill learning and physical involvement coincide with steady rates of change? Is weight gain attributable to puppy fat alone, and how does a child's build compare with its friends?

•   Activities which involve the large muscle groups of the body burn more calories than those where the body is supported. Try to encourage children to walk for extending periods of time, and to run at a higher pace until they start to breathe more quickly; also encourage cycling and swimming.

## Changes in Body Proportions

The uneven nature of child growth extends to the long limbs of the body, so important in producing and controlling movement skills. Thus the growth of the arms, legs and trunk in height, breadth and mass follows a particular pattern which is directly linked to the nature of general bone development, and as such is worthy of note.

Whilst most people are aware that bone growth precedes muscle development, not all are aware that bone itself develops from another substance. The long levers have a central segment of fully formed bone, whilst the extremities are often made up of hard attaching outcrops, growth plates and softer cartilage awaiting the developmental change of structure known as ossification. X-rays, though now known to be unsafe if given too often, are nevertheless a good indication of this developmental process, and allow the age of a child to be estimated on the basis of bone maturity alone. Such studies suggest that all 629 bones are not fully ossified until some time between twenty-one and twenty-five years of age, though this process is determined largely by inherited potential.

This means that the softer segments of bone do not have either the constituents or the capabilities of the finished form, and so may be affected one way or another by external influence. Thus, some loading of naive cartilaginous bones is likely to have a positive strengthening effect on both their cross-sectional composition and their normal elongation — indeed supervised, controlled and progressive strength training, using bodyweight and gravity as the initial resistance in building an endurance base, are essential if children are to have sufficient strength in relatively weak body parts to cope with the technical requirements of sports and activities which have a young competitive start. It is also worth noting that heavy loading — for example, carrying maximal amounts on the shoulders — is more likely to cause yielding and bending rather than cracking and breaking as would be expected in more mature injuries. Placing the emphasis on increasing control over the body in a variety of novel exercise situations, for an increased period of time, is therefore an acceptable focus so that strength levels can keep pace with the technical skills they support. Finding programmes and coaches who understand chilren's strength potential and requirements thus becomes the key to ensuring that the experience is both pleasurable and profitable.

## Temporary Loss of Ability

The growth plates — or epiphyseal joints as they are known — allow the majority of growth in a limb to develop in certain directions, and in balance with the growth potential at other extremities. This is sensible, and the child can therefore learn to control its overall change in height in an ongoing way. Nevertheless, temporary losses of ability can be directly associated with this proportional growth process, and require greater consideration in relation to muscle growth. Suffice it to say that informed and sensitive counselling can help prepare children for the specific changes anticipated so that they do not have an adverse reaction at a time when emotionally they are not always mature enough to be able to cope with unexpected change.

Whilst the long-term effect of high doses of external loading on these sites continues to be debated, there is no doubt that they are susceptible to chemical influence. Functional loss — that is, a premature end to growth and a diminished final stature — are two of the known outcomes where drugs, particularly those which enhance performance, are involved.

When observing and measuring middle years' children, most growth will occur at certain points and in line with statistical expectations. For example in the legs, most of the growth emanates from epiphyseal plates above and below the knee, with 70 per cent change in the femur (hip bone) expected above the knee, and the remainder occurring in the pelvic joint. This suggests that when compared to, say, a period six months before, the knee will have experienced great change in its immediate vicinity without a corresponding increase in muscular strength and control. This means that high-impact activities requiring repeated stops, starts and turns will be problematic, particularly if they are performed on an unforgiving surface, as is often the case. The dilemma lies in the fact that whilst the child needs to relearn how to perform such movements now that its body has grown, it probably does not have the muscular strength to control such movements without some possibility of adverse reaction occurring. The main suggestion here must be that it is safer to concentrate on the quality and variation of fewer movements. Moreover, too much unsupervised practice may be harmful, particularly if it is done on surfaces that contribute to joint attrition.

## Training Tips

•   The composition of bones changes throughout a child's life. Check that children are not being asked to carry excessive loads on their shoulders, to walk or run too far whilst loaded up, or to do too many sprint starts or fast turns on hard surfaces.

•   Do not leave strengthening exercise to chance. Progressive work which takes into account body weight in relation to endurance strength will provide an interesting challenge whilst increasing bone and muscle strength at the same time. Mix up skills with strengthening so that both develop in tandem.

•   Remember that involvement should reflect learning skills, it should be fun, and you should feel good about yourself. Select programmes where training is given in small doses to supplement the overall experience. Look for coaches who understand exercise appropriate for children, and ask what you could do to help them when playing in the park, pool or gym.

## New Bodies, Different Abilities

The notion that children are all arms and legs at this stage, and prone to be gangly, awkward and clumsy at times, appears to be equally applicable to boys and to girls. A quite common pattern is that the trunk and the legs grow longer fairly rapidly, then the trunk becomes broader, and the feet increase in size to counterbalance the increased overall height. Children now start approaching two-thirds of final adult height averages. The increasingly perceptible differences between boys and girls have some basis in their future adult roles: thus whilst girls are, on average, the same height as, or slightly taller than boys, they now start to develop a lighter, more smoothly edged pelvis which is destined to be wider and have a bigger internal cavity than that in boys. The implications for birthing potential are obvious, but this widening of the hips also has significant importance for exercise and sport. From nine to 14.5 years, the hips continue to grow laterally, and slowly become as wide as, and then wider than the upper thigh. This gradual development of female shape alters the way in which the large muscles of the thigh attach to the hip; this in turn has the effect of increasing stability and flexibility whilst at the same time reducing stride length.

Boys are not as affected by hip enlargement, but instead they experience a change inherited from forefathers used to a much harsher physical lifestyle: thus it seems possible that the increase in size of male shoulders, proportional to head width, is linked to the hunter/fisher lifestyles of previous eras. Whatever the basis, the longer upper limbs, functional elbow complex and larger shoulders — later to provide the base for strong, well integrated muscles — now allow for far greater force of movement to be generated. Pulling, gripping and pushing all start to become much more developed, and objects can be thrown with much greater velocity than before.

These changing body proportions now need to be taught effective techniques in conjunction with appropriate strengthening programmes.

## Training Tips

•   Where boys gain in strength and size, they tend to lose in flexibility, and on a more temporary basis co-ordination and agility. They need to develop improved ranges of movement to keep pace with size changes, whilst at the same time returning  to practise skills, in more advanced form, that were previously well learned but are now proving difficult to control. The sense organs in the head are now further away from limbs which carry out the movements, making relearning all the more necessary.

•   Girls' hips start to widen, from the age of nine, to a point where their physical abilities will change. Movements requiring flexibility, agility, hand—feet co-ordination are potentially easier for them to control, and if practised, can be a source of personal achievement and enhanced self-belief. Upper body skills will not change that quickly, but will eventually start to compare less favourably than boys. They need to be given more practice for improvement to occur.

•   Boys' loss of flexibility starts to become apparent. Select coaches and teachers who support the notion of stretching as a means of adopting useful lifeskills and as preparation for later involvement where warming up will become crucial.

•   Whilst boys' throwing prowess improves, their agility, hand—foot co-ordination, turning and balance may change, particularly in those who approach the growth spurt before their contemporaries. Coaches would be advised to discuss how physical changes affect physical actions: in this way they can help to sustain motivation and can provide purpose to independent learners.

## The Good and the Not So Good

The prepubertal child has the energy and drive to learn most new things put its way, but some activities can be predicted to cause more difficulty than they need to.

Middle school children come in all shapes and sizes, but generally do not have much in the way of noticeable muscle mass. The latter provides the athletic ability to do sports and activities that require speed and power, but it does not start to develop until hormonal changes intervene after puberty. This presents an interesting situation for the person charged with selecting activities for children, in that the skills of certain sports often inspire and motivate children to organize recreational  games, but the successful performance of those skills relies on muscle power that they do not have. Therefore training to develop ball skill and movement efficiency should have a higher priority than explosive fitness training, which should not be given too much emphasis.

### *Running*

Running is the basis of most of the sports which are played in this country, and it is an important area for development. Children nearly always learn a

*Young athletes develop their running skills.*

technique which suits them, often through trial and error, and without too much expert instruction. They generally use this technique to run in the same way, regardless of whether sprint or endurance ability is needed — basically they are runners before they specialize. At this time, coaches and teachers can usefully spend a small amount of activity time practising running in a tall position with relaxed shoulders, rangy leg action, and arms and knees which lift in line so that all the propulsion allows forward movement.

## The Training Surface

Having mentioned the adverse effects of very hard surfaces on developing bodies, two related issues should be mentioned. Coaches and teachers are well placed to log how much time children play per week, and on what type of surface. This is important because, as we shall see in later sections, injury is often caused through over-use. Also, children who play games on large pitches for schools, clubs and weekend sides each week could be playing too much — although without keeping a diary this is difficult to evaluate.

• Encourage training on grass or on wooden sprung floors as in school gymnasiums; the time spent playing on synthetic surfaces should be limited to competition.

## Training Shoes

It is also important to keep a check on the type and condition of the training shoes that children wear. The brand and the price matter little when compared with the protective features which should be provided — and looked for — in a good pair of trainers. Most of these shoes have either a leather or a man-made upper: leather ones provide greater protection for the feet where frequent turning, stopping, kicking or hitting — as in hockey — is necessary; however, nylon-type uppers are recommended for sports involving straight line forward movement, as in endurance running, jogging or sprinting. More specifically, the following need to be considered:

• The shoe should have a strong toe box which will protect the toes and nails during contact.

• The laces should have a padded tongue so that the soft tissue around the arch of the foot is not injured.

• A sole which is robust and has a slightly higher heel than toe will take pressure off the Achilles heel and aid balance when running.

• Avoid hard heel tabs, especially ones which are unnecessarily raised, as this can cause discomfort when sprinting and turning.

## Training Tips for the Coach

Whilst the health-giving benefits of sport and exercise are well known, children cannot be motivated by such long-term goals. They need to experience play with a fitness element so that they can enjoy the process of exercise and the positive feelings that accompany it. This can be assisted by the following training ploys:

• Make fitness activities fun — try relating them to some game or outcome. Running with a purpose — such as to a certain point, to avoid being caught, or as a means of scoring points — replaces negative sensations and thoughts of fatigue with the positive desire to achieve success in the chosen game. It is vital that the child is able to experience that warm, rewarding feeling of well-being which immediately follows the completion of steady sustained exercise, rather than succumbing to feelings of tiredness and pain.

• When working with young children, use the warm-up as the time to establish sustained movement, rather than having too many aerobic training sessions. The warm-up is deliberately non-competitive, it establishes a routine which is applicable to any sport the children may try later in life, and it needs whole body movement prior to muscle stretching. This is the time to practise running forwards, backwards and sideways as well as twisting, skipping, turning and returning to running from associated game-related situations.

• Remember that children heat up and cool down much more quickly than adults, regardless of the ambient temperature. Their sweating mechanism is still under-developed, which makes it difficult for them to cope with excesses of heat. In real terms this means they will need to have shorter, less intensive running and stretching sessions. It also means that the effect of the warm-up will wear off more quickly, and that another warm-up will be needed, typically after 15mins of standing still, watching or listening to instruction. When the weather is hot coaches should have water on hand, and should avoid working for too long with young children. A water break is more likely to improve performance than simply continuing with the same practice.

• Coaches and teachers who analyse the skills and techniques of activities have a better basis for practising the elements that children can pick up well. Skills need to be constantly revisited so that children are confident of being able to execute them.

Sessions which allow children to learn and practise movements, and which include just some elements of fitness training towards the end, are more appropriate to a child's perceptions of why it is present and what it wants to achieve.

## The Parental Role

Children need regular opportunities to be involved in sport, and participation in a wide variety of activities remains the central developmental goal. This means selecting activities on the basis of what desirable skills they include, how challenging is the environment in which they operate, and how much scope there is for continued improvement and progression. Those which stress body control — such as swimming, gymnastics and movement games — should be selected first, ahead of those which also require ball control. Children can be effectively introduced to these more advanced activities in play situations with their parents, before they begin more formal attendance at clubs and classes.

• Observe a child's quality of movement, and ask simple questions such as how well they thought they had done, and what they could do to improve their performance. This can be done whilst watching other children moving on television programmes prior to trying the same types of activity at home.

• Buy a book on child development and produce a list of fundamental movement skills. Think about how these may be organized so that the simpler ones are attempted first. Consider how these might be varied to impose greater challenge.

• Some investment in equipment may be useful. Good starters would be a skipping rope, an aerobic bouncer, a balance board and a log, an extending bar to wedge in a door frame, and a climbing rope or pole. An exercise mat for stretching and strengthening, a hoop and a set of small plastic cones can also be acquired without undue expense, often second hand. All would encourage whole body exercise with an elevated heart rate, but some degree of adult supervision would be necessary.

• To improve water confidence try using a leg float, goggles and a snorkel; these are all short-term aids which should help in achieving the correct body and head alignment. Similarly a hollow rubber ball or replica mammal can be used to encourage initial distance swimming — making a game of it will help the child cover a realistic distance without feeling stressed about it. Light, bright-coloured objects which sink can serve a purpose when teaching children to swim underwater and to make surface dives. Masks may be used at bath time to help children get used to having their faces in the water.

• Running games on grass in the garden are simple to set up — for instance, moving objects from one place to another, whilst negotiating low-level challenges along the way to test agility. Hop-scotch may be more appropriate for a yard area.

The progression to skills requiring a greater degree of hand—eye coordination, concentration and technical ability can also be best developed at home to begin

*A child showing good hand – eye coordination.*

with. Often a child can be helped — as long as it is willing to accept advice! — by making just small adjustments in the timing of when they do things, or in the positioning of their body in relation to the ball or racket or whatever is the games object.

• Every child has a dominant eye, hand and foot: watch each child carefully to establish which this is, because it will affect how they line up prior to performing a movement.

• Watch a number of times to obtain a consistent image of how a child is performing a particular skill. Consider how easy or difficult they are accomplishing it by looking at how they prepare to throw, catch, hit or kick. Can it be made less complicated by reducing the number of things they have to control?

• Is the equipment suitable for them to have the best chance of success? Balls are graded for size commensurate with age and the size of hands and feet. A medium-weight ball, often on a rope or string for hitting and kicking, maximizes a child's chance of making a good first contact.

• An easily identified, bright and safe target will help increase accuracy and consistency. Whilst not everyone wants lines painted on their exterior walls, the use of cones or posts to make goals, archery targets to throw at, and adjustable netball and basketball hoops, greatly increases motivation and provides plenty of variety in practice sessions.

• By altering your position in relation to the child, they learn to control and send an object with increased accuracy and a shorter overall performance time. By counting out the number of passes or shots in a rally they learn to concentrate on a clean contact, without having to remind themselves to watch the ball. These small learning games make their abilities much more relevant to competitive games later on.

• Add movements before and after skills once an acceptable level of understanding of the task has been established.

## Expert Assistance

Enlisting the help of a coach or teacher is the next logical step in maintaining and broadening the development achieved within the family. The use of a specialist area with ancillary facilities, the chance to work with other children, the wearing of sportskit, and being involved in enticing practices are all good reasons for taking part in such activities — but primarily it is the decision to be guided by an expert that makes it a new departure. But what are parents buying into when they take up such a relationship?

The rewards of such involvement include having children work with some-one who likes and understands them at their stage of development. The activi-ty leader coach or teacher should have both experience and knowledge of the developmental processes that children are going through, and should be able to select appropriate exercise. A child-centred approach, with learning, fun and achievement as the main objectives, is central to the success of such pro-grammes.

It is also essential that they can select easy ways of introducing new activi-ties, and that they know how to get children over the sticking points that such learning brings with it. This may be caused by mental fatigue, dehydration, physical tiredness, frustration or boredom — but the important thing is that they recognize the symptoms and change the activity before interest and achievement are lost.

• Check that they teach the children rather than just coach the activity

• Ask how much progress they note and expect over a given period

• Do not just drop the children off, but stay and watch. You can check such things as safety, discipline, rapport and equality of opportunity, whilst your children can show you what they have learned.

• Ask how you can support what they are doing with the coach.

During these skill-hungry years children will have high aspirations, although it may not be long before these ambitions are lost. However, by teaching them a wide range of foundation skills and making them feel good about their achieve-ments, children will be better prepared to consider more adult sports, and will be equipped with a better basis for later specialization.

# CHAPTER FIVE

# Are We Having Fun Yet?

As children progress through the primary years many issues will arise that will directly influence their level of participation in sport. Moreover these years are critical in determining whether they develop a liking for sport, which will remain with them for the rest of their lives.

This chapter will explore a number of areas within the realms of sport psychology that will provide us with a clearer understanding as to why children participate in sport.

## Motivation

It is fundamental to the coaching process to discover why children actually do participate in sport. In essence they fall into three groups, each with distinct differences in terms of their participation motives: firstly, those who participate on a regular basis; secondly, those who used to participate in sport but have dropped out; and thirdly, those who have never taken part in sport other than at school as part of the national curriculum. Knowing why they do, or do not, enjoy their sport is crucial to the development of coaching schemes, coaching methods and coaching knowledge. Thus the emphasis on coaching programmes should be to keep children involved in sport by fulfilling their participation motives, whatever they may be. However, before exploring these motives, let us take a closer look at the concept of motivation.

Motivation is one of those words frequently used within sport that can describe very different things. Consider the following examples: a coach of elite basketball players says after losing a hard match that his team wasn't motivated. Next, a recreational football team has a poor showing at training, and the coach's explanation is that the players weren't motivated. Clearly in these two examples the behaviour that is being described is very different, yet the same terminology is used, and it is this which can be confusing.

Psychologists have investigated motivation for many years, and many different theoretical perspectives have emerged. As regards understanding the sport context, a cognitive approach, rather than an emotional one, is considered to be the most beneficial — in broad terms, motivation is deemed to be the internal process that guides, activates and maintains an individual's behaviour over time. It is seen to have three distinct behavioural components to it:

selection, persistence and intensity (Gould, 1984), and each has different behavioural consequences which need to be explored.

## Selection

Selection is related to how attractive an activity appears to be from the individual's perspective. So why do some children choose football whilst others choose
swimming? In the first instance there has to be something inherently attractive
about the sport to capture a child's imagination and to make them want to take
part. Clearly this is going to vary greatly from one child to another, and will
depend on a number of factors including family background, school, exposure
through the mass media, to name a few. But it is worth remembering that if you
want to interest children, and more importantly their parents, in taking part in
your activity, you need to make it attractive.

## Persistence

The second aspect of motivation is persistence, and it refers to an individual's
desire to continue with a given activity. In terms of the sporting context, do the
children stay on the programme once they have signed up for it, or do you
experience a high drop-out rate?

## Intensity

Lastly there is intensity, which refers to the behavioural component best
described as effort: that is, how hard does an individual try when engaged in
any given activity? From a coaching perspective it is clear that some children
are taking part in your activity because they are intrinsically gaining something
from the experience — generally these are the children who are attentive, work
hard in the sessions and who make the most progress. However, there are also
children who seem to take only a limited part in the activity, and who do not
put a lot of effort into what they are doing.

If we return to the initial examples, it is clear that the first coach is referring
to a problem of intensity, whilst that of the second coach relates to persistence.
These distinctions are very helpful to the development of effective coaching
programmes that can address all the behavioural aspects of motivation. This
will be discussed in more detail later in this chapter when the role of goal-setting is considered.

We must now address our original question of understanding why
children participate in sport, why they do not participate, and why they withdraw. A considerable amount of research has been undertaken in this area,
much of it motivated by concern over the apparent decline in children's active
participation in sport, and concomitant with this, the seriously detrimental
effect on health that a sedentary lifestyle can have — a nation of 'couch pota-
toes' is not an ideal vision for the future. This research does seem to imply that

an adult's pattern of behaviour, be it active or sedentary, is established early on in life.

## Why do Children Participate?

The research mentioned above indicates that children have multiple motives for participating in sport, the main ones being: for the fun it promises; for the enjoyment of the excitement; the mastery of skills; getting in shape; because they enjoy teamwork; and because they want to be physically active, and to learn new skills

*Children enjoying the different challenges of balancing.*

It also indicates that the three key motives of having fun, mastery of skills, and being part of a team are of paramount importance to the young participant in sport, and that its being fun is pivotal. Clearly this is something that should be carefully noted. What is also interesting to note is that 'winning' does not feature as being a key motive for participation — perhaps this is an adult projection that we place upon children.

## Why do they Not Participate?

If these are the reasons why children do participate, we should also consider why children withdraw, or never participate at all. Again, there is useful research in this area to draw upon, namely that the most frequently cited reasons by both groups of children are: I am not very good at it; I am not as good as other children; I'd rather be with my friends; I lose; I don't learn new skills very well; it is too serious; I am not noticed when I do sport; it isn't fun; it hurts; I have homework to do.

## Why do Children Withdraw from Sport?

It would appear that the principal motive for withdrawal is centred on a child's perception of its own competence. Thus for such a child, participation in sport is fuelling negative emotions and low self-esteem, and the question that has to be asked is whether or not the coaching methods that he is experiencing contribute to this. In many instances I consider this is the case, and that the coaching style adopted by a coach can have a direct influence on all aspects of motivation demonstrated by the children participating (this will be further examined a little later in this chapter).

With regard to the above, it is clear that the perceived ability or the competence of the children is critical in determining their participation in sport. For the more able children, the feeling of being able to accomplish and master sports skills is a powerful motivator. In contrast, the withdrawers and non-participants find that their perceived lack of ability, real or otherwise, directly contributes to their attrition from sport. This notion is reflected in Harter's competence motivation theory which states that individuals are motivated to demonstrate competence — in other words, children who are high in perceived physical competence are more likely to participate in sport than children who are not.

Research indicates that there are significant differences between participants, withdrawers and non-participants in relation to perceived physical competence, with the non-participants demonstrating the lowest levels. This research also indicates that these groups of children have had very different experiences when participating in sport. Thus the children who continue to participate have had positive feedback on their skill mastery attempts, and have had a good time doing it; this has in turn made them feel good about themselves, promoting positive self-image and self-esteem, all-important to the developing child. On the other hand, the children who drop out of sport are more likely to have experienced unfavourable competence judgements, and to have suffered a negative emotional response as a result of participating. This type of experience can be potentially very damaging to the fragile ego of the developing child, and unfortunately could well discourage all future participation.

## Self-Esteem in Sport

This relationship between self-esteem and participation in sport has been further investigated, and findings indicate that children who participate in sport have improved self-image as compared to children who do not. So the children who do not participate are missing opportunities to develop both physically and psychologically. Clearly sport can provide the opportunity for all children to feel good about themselves, to achieve goals, maintain health and develop skills — as long as the sporting environment allows this to happen.

A further distinction exists between girls and boys, with boys' physical ability being more readily perceived, on average, than that of girls. This difference is reflected in the numbers of girls that participate in sport as compared to boys, and it is something that needs to be addressed if we are to encourage all children to adopt a healthy lifestyle that incorporates participation in sport.

## Motivation: Some General Rules

So the question is, what can coaches, teachers and parents do to encourage young children to participate in sport outside the limited national curriculum PE? Let us examine some of the ways in which one can influence the motivation of children to participate; the following are some very general rules:

• Ensure that activities are FUN. This sounds easy, but you have to consider the activity from the child's perspective, because their concept of fun and yours may be quite different. Be sure to listen to feedback from them regarding the different activities that you do.

• Emphasize competence and personal success. This can be done most effectively through goal-setting (see below).

• Provide great variety in training sessions, thus allowing children to experience a wide range of skills. This will also provide more opportunity for them to experience success.

• Do reward effort rather than just outcome

• Ensure that all children receive both verbal and non-verbal praise. Sometimes we forget that actions speak louder than words.

• Allow the children to be part of the decision-making process. This might seem strange — how can a seven-year-old possibly know what to do? Surely that is the job of the adult? However, by encouraging personal responsibility you will also be enhancing motivation, and this will then be reflected in their intrinsic desire to continue to take part. Tasks involving such responsibility might range from choosing specific activities to taking care of their sports environment.

• Give rewards that relate to performance, rather than to outcome. On this basis every child will be sure of some reward.

• Do set performance goals.

Effective goal-setting will ensuring that children not only enjoy their sport, but also remain involved; it can transform any coaching session.

## Effective Goal-Setting

The benefits of goal-setting on performance have been shown to be effective in a number of arenas including sports participation, and there is conclusive evidence from a broad spectrum of research that it does work. However, like motivation, goal-setting terminology is frequently banded about in sport but is often poorly applied, and this is especially true in sports programmes for young children. First we need to consider the benefits of goal-setting with particular reference to motivation.

Goal-setting works because:

1. It directs children's attention and action (i.e. selectivity motivation).
2. It prolongs effort (i.e. persistence motivation).
3. It mobilizes energy expenditure (i.e. intensity motivation).
4. It creates the development of a motivation strategy (i.e. selectivity, persistence and intensity).

These factors are the essence of motivated behaviour, which is desirable in any child who is participating in sport. Through the achievement of goals a coach will find that the following improvements also take place (Martens, 1987):

1. Performance improves.
2. The quality of training improves.
3. Expectations are clarified.
4. Boredom is reduced.
5. Self-confidence, satisfaction and pride are developed.
6  The intrinsic motivation to achieve is improved.

This sounds a little bit like magic, and one wonders if all this can really be achieved with the simple application of goal-setting? And the answer really is yes, as long as it is done effectively, and this requires careful thought and deliberation. So the question is HOW?

## Space Map

There are some clear steps that can be followed that will make the process much more effective, and these can be applied to any group of children participating at any level. The easy way to remember them is via the mnemonic SPACE MAP:

**S***pecific:*  Ensure that when you are setting goals with your athletes it is very clear exactly what is being asked and how these goals are going to be achieved. Goals which are vague in nature, such as 'Do your best', allow for great ambiguity, and can result in a child not really knowing if it has actually achieved the goal or not. Work with goals that are clearly defined and measurable, then the young athlete will know exactly when he has reached his goal, and so will gain self-satisfaction coupled with recognized levels of competence.

**P***articipation:*  Allow the children to be part of the goal-setting process. Research indicates that goals are much more likely to be attained if the individual has a personal investment in the goal being set — and don't underestimate the ability of even very young children to cope with this. With careful consideration of the child's maturity, this process can work very well. It will also create a feeling of personal responsibility for the outcome, so you will be enhancing the potential for personal achievement. This in turn will directly affect the motivation levels of the children participating in your sport.

**A***bsolute:*  These are goals that have a defined outcome over which the individual can have control.

**C***ombined:*  It is most effective to combine short-term goals with long-term goals: the long-term goal encourages ambition, whilst the short-term goal ensures the satisfaction of small achievements along the way. This method will help to increase persistence, because the child has something to aim for, and intensity due to the success of mastering the small steps en route to the big goal.  Long-term goals are often too far in the future to motivate immediate action, whereas short-term goals allow performance evaluation, and will further enhance motivation as progress towards the long-term goal is perceived.

**E***valuated:*  For goals to be effective there must be some evaluation procedure which measures achievement. There is no point in setting goals with your athletes if their progress isn't regularly evaluated: it is evaluation that makes goal-setting work. The ways in which a goal is going to be assessed must be clear to the children because this can vary enormously, from a small evaluation of each session to show what needs to be worked on in order to pass to the next step, to a full assessment possibly using a formal award scheme — these exist within many sports.

*Moderate:*  The setting of moderate goals is necessary for the greatest achievement motivation. Thus, if the goal set is too difficult the probability of success is low, and this is more likely to demotivate. On the other hand if the goal is too easy, then the incentive value of success is low. It is clear that establishing the correct balance between challenge and success will lead to moderate goals: the challenge for the coach is to ensure that all children's needs are met in the goal-setting process. Moreover, all goals must be appropriate for each individual.

*Assessment:*  Before any goals can be set, there has to be some assessment to determine exactly the current strengths and weaknesses of the child. This can be done in a number of ways — some objective, others subjective — whereby the child is asked how it perceives its own ability.

Public:  When goals are set in a public arena they are more likely to be adhered to. (The same basic principle is applied in Weight Watchers, and we know how successful they are!) The key is to present this in a supportive manner, so the more able children in the group will appreciate those who are less able, and who will be working to achieve different aims. Thus all children will be given the opportunity to feel that they are achieving a level of competence.

## The Pro-Forma

One of the simplest ways of incorporating all of the above is to develop simple pro-formas that can be adapted to suit the needs of your sport and the level of the children you are working with. These can be developed to meet the needs of very young children, mixed abilities and all sports. Once the basic principle is understood the application is simple. Opposite is an example of a pro-forma that can be used. It was designed for seven-year-olds taking part in a recreational football programme.

ACHIEVEMENT RECORD FOR ................

| Skills: | Running | Kicking | Jumping | Ball skills | Listening | Concentrating | Passing | Teamwork | Hopping |
|---|---|---|---|---|---|---|---|---|---|
| How good am I?<br>Very good<br>Good<br>Quite good<br>Not very good |  |  |  |  |  |  |  |  |  |
| COACH ASSESSMENT |  |  |  |  |  |  |  |  |  |

<u>My Goals for this term are:</u>

1
2
3
4

| How am I doing? | wk1 | wk2 | wk3 | wk4 | wk5 | wk6 | wk7 | wk8 | wk9 | k10 |
|---|---|---|---|---|---|---|---|---|---|---|
| Better | | | | | | | | | | |
| Same | | | | | | | | | | |
| Worse | | | | | | | | | | |
| Goals achieved: | | | | | wk5 | | | | wk10 | |

Signed by:
Date:

Athlete          Coach          Parent

The pro-forma can be used in the following way:

STEP ONE: Identify the skills that your group will be working on. These will be sport- and level-specific. If you are coaching a recreational class you might have a range of abilities within the group; consequently it might be appropriate to have different achievement records that identify slightly different skills. Ensure that you include a range of skills: these can be behaviour skills as well as physical and technical skills.

STEP TWO: Ask the children to assess their own ability on each of the skills and write it on the form: 'very good', 'good' and so on.

STEP THREE: The coach assesses the children's ability. You can use a range of means to do this, from simple skills' tests, physical assessment and observation. Write it on the form using the same language, and keep it very simple.

STEP FOUR: Work with the children to set their goals for the term, or the length of time that is most appropriate. Ensure that these are going to be worked within your plan for the programme. You will now have children who will be identifying different skills to develop. Try to get a range of goals set i.e. technical, physical and behaviour goals.

STEP FIVE: Allow the children enough time to evaluate their performance after each session. This should not take very long!

STEP SIX: Evaluate the goals formally at the mid-point in the programme as well as at the end. You can instigate reward schemes to complement the goal-setting. For example, if a child attains one goal they get a red star, two goals a blue star, three goals a silver star, and gold if all the goals are achieved. Because the children are trying to achieve different goals they can all be successful.

## Effort: What is it?

Clearly if any goals are to be achieved the children must put in some effort. This is a fairly simple concept for adults to understand, namely if you work hard at any given activity you will be likely to succeed, and if you don't try then you won't. The notion of ability is a part of this, too: as adults we recognize that we have greater ability in some areas than in others; consequently, some things we can do with apparent ease and minimum effort, whilst other things require a lot of hard work before we achieve our goal. This is not the case with children, who have very different perceptions regarding ability and effort, which changes with age. It is worth considering this relationship in more detail, as it will be critical in understanding their approach to any given task:

**2—4yrs** Children will feel able if they can master a given task. They operate from an egocentric perspective, meaning that they don't compare themselves to other people. Consequently they set their own standards for judging how hard a task is, and what success is. This of course can be very different from the adult view.

**4—6yrs** Children will now assess ability in terms of objective outcomes e.g. jumping to a fixed point. There is a shift in their perceptions of task difficulty, which is related to the outcome, so they will think that a task is easy if the outcome is achieved often. Children at this age make no distinction between effort and ability: if a skill requires more effort, then they perceive their own ability to be greater.

**6—7yrs** Children now start to bring others into the equation in order to determine their own ability. Ability is perceived as accomplishing tasks that not many people can do. Therefore, if everyone can do a skill it is not seen as being 'hard' or needing any great ability. Ability is being able to do what most people cannot do.

**7—9yrs** Children now perceive success as being directly linked to effort. The harder you try, the more success you should have. They are not really aware of ability as being a limiting factor to success.

**9—10yrs** Children will now begin to distinguish between effort and ability: an interpretation of success without trying is that they must have better ability.

**11—12+yrs** It is only now that children fully understand that ability is something separate from effort. They will increasingly compare themselves to other people as a means of determining their own ability.

These stages of understanding as experienced by children are critical when trying to develop effective goal-setting programmes. It requires great skill on the part of the coach to consider not only the key aspects of goal-setting, but also to ensure that it is commensurate with the child's stage of cognitive development. However, if these concepts are taken on board, everyone will benefit.

## Coaching Styles and the Young Athlete

We have discussed in detail elements relating specifically to children and their participation in sport, but we now need to turn our attention to coaches. A coach's personality does not appear to be critical with regard to his effectiveness, and indeed many different personality types are good coaches — you only have to consider Arsene Wenger and Alex Ferguson to realize that they are very different types of people, yet both are very effective coaches. So clearly there has to be something else that makes a good coach, and research in this area indicates very strongly that it is the behaviour of the coach — what he actually does — that is critical. Key research by Chelladurai and Saleh (1980) identified five distinct behaviours exhibited by coaches, namely:

1.   Training and instruction behaviour:  directed towards improving technical and physical performance.
2.   Democratic behaviour:  allows for participation by athletes in the decision-making process.
3.   Autocratic behaviour:  behaviour by the coach that removes participation by the athletes in any decisions.
4.   Social support behaviour:  shows genuine care and concern for the athletes as individual people.
5.   Rewarding behaviour:  positively rewards the athletes by recognizing good performance and effort.

The critical question then is, how much of any given behaviour is going to be effective for the group of children that I am working with? To answer this we need to consider the interaction that exists in any coaching situation between the coach, the athlete and the situation — only in this way can a complete picture of effective coaching behaviour patterns be established. So let us consider each of these elements in turn.

*A coach demonstrates good training and instruction behaviour.*

## The Athlete

This book has adopted a developmental perspective when considering the coaching process, but this does not simply reflect the chronological age of a child. Take, for example, an international junior gymnast aged twelve, and a beginner basketball player aged sixteen, and you will see that age alone does not give a true picture in determining what each needs from a coach: the athlete's ability and experience must be taken into account too. In combination these constitute the 'athletic maturity' of the child, and it is this which should dictate the behavioural pattern adopted by the coach. Research would indicate that when the maturity levels are low the athlete requires low task behaviour and high social support behaviour. When the athlete is high in athletic maturity (i.e. national/international standard) the same is true. However, when the athlete is at an intermediate stage of development the opposite appears to be true.

The most notable research in this area is by Smith and Smoll (1993), and it has particular reference to children; it also emphasizes the importance of behaviour that is positively rewarding and gives social support to the children. It observes that coaches who adopt this type of behaviour nearly always find that young athletes feel encouraged to participate because they experience greater satisfaction, higher self-esteem, better self-image and lower anxiety. When questioned, children liked their coaches more and had a greater liking for the sport with which they were involved. Thus we might conclude that for coaches who adopt this coaching behaviour this ultimately results in lower drop-out rates.

Clearly there is a powerful message emanating from this area of research, indicating that 'It ain't what you do — it's the way that you do it' that is important. Sometimes coaches are actually not very good at recognizing their own behaviour, so it is useful to get feedback from the children they work with, or they could ask a colleague to observe one of their sessions and get feedback that way. And for all coaches, don't be afraid to change: you might find that you have more to offer than you previously thought.

## The Coach

The style that a coach adopts in her sessions — democratic or autocratic — is almost bound to have an influence on the motivation levels of the participants. Sport has traditionally been associated with an autocratic style of leadership whereby the athletes are 'told' what to do by the coach: they have little or no input in the process. As regards training, competition and lifestyle the coach makes all the decisions: she is seen to be all-knowing and all-powerful, the athletes her subordinates. Given that many coaches replicate the style that they were coached in, it is not surprising that this approach is commonplace; indeed many coaches are very comfortable adopting this style, and it might be the reason why they became coaches. The question that needs to be asked is whether this style is always appropriate when coaching young athletes.

Research into this area suggests a number of things. Firstly, it is clear from the previous section on motivation that if an athlete is part of the goal-setting, and therefore the decision-making process, this will enhance her self-image and increase intrinsic motivation; a completely autocratic style would prevent this from happening. A democratic style means that any decisions will be arrived at jointly, allowing for better communication and cohesion amongst the athletes.

However, an autocratic approach allows for speed of decision-making, which can be critical in sport; it also allows for the total responsibility to rest with the coach. This may appeal to some athletes who perhaps do not want to be part of this process so long as the coach is seen to be 'getting it right'.

The message that emerges is that the coach must be flexible. Thus at times an autocratic approach is the most appropriate to be effective, but at others a democratic style is best, and the coach needs to be sensitive to changing conditions and to alter their behaviour accordingly. It must be remembered that coaching is a two-way interactional process with both athlete and coach contributing — and coaches can forget this, and treat the children as simply passive receivers of information and instruction. In fact the coaching style they adopt will greatly influence a child's perception. As we have said, all coaches will generally adopt a style that suits them, and many will coach in the way that they were coached. However, it is necessary for them to reflect upon this to be sure that they are meeting the needs of the children.

## The Situation

The last element to be considered is the situation within which the athletes and coach come together. Different sports have very different characteristics and consequently will place different demands on both the coach and the athlete. Some of these distinctions can be quite simple, as between team or individual sports, indoor and outdoor sports, competitive or recreational.

The above factors will be critical in determining the most effective coaching style.

## The Interaction

It is only by considering all the above elements and how they impinge on one another that truly effective coaching can be achieved. There are many different ways to coach young children, and these will depend on a number of different factors including the personality and behaviour of the coach, the situation, and the athletes themselves. This approach to understanding effective coaching has been termed interactional, and its nature ultimately determines the satisfaction of the athletes and the performance outcomes. If there is conflict between the actual behaviour of the coach and the preferred behaviour, this will result in dissatisfaction, and the consequences of this could be that either the athletes or the coach withdraw from the situation. Performance can also suffer, and coaches need to recognize that they are part of the performance outcome; thus if a team is not doing well, then clearly the coach must have something to do with this. Unfortunately many coaches do not accept this, and will simply blame the team. In the final analysis, however, the quality of the relationships will determine the outcome.

When coaches are working with this young age group it is important that they develop a positive and effective coaching style that embraces all the individuals and gives them more than simply the skills of the sport.

# CHAPTER SIX

# Grow Your Own Superstar

This chapter considers issues which relate to being gifted at sport at an early age. Key factors include how potentially talented young performers can be recognized, and what spotters of such talent look for when selecting elite groups.

Sport in the UK is in crisis, and national performance over the last decade has been increasingly disappointing; where once we dominated we are now being overshadowed, as was demonstrated only too clearly at the Atlanta Games in 1996 where we finished thirtieth on the medal table. Moreover, in sports which were once seen to be the sole domain of British athletes, we are struggling: poor performances in cricket seem to be commonplace; in football, the best British team only got into the second round in the last World Cup — rather unimpressive when you consider that it is the national game. So how can we account for these performances?

The women and men who are the elite athletes of today owe their success — or lack of it — to a system that began to develop their talent ten years ago. This is clearly where the problem lies, and the deficiencies of that system have been emerging over the last few years; by comparison, other countries have researched and developed much more effective methods to select and train those athletes with the best potential ability, with impressive results.

Selection for elite sport is happening for athletes at an increasingly young age — in many sports there are national squads in operation for nine- to ten-year-olds, and some pro football clubs have reportedly signed up seven-year-olds: this reflects world-wide practice, and in a number of sports coaches are having to search for very young talent because of the reducing age of elite performers. The average age for elite female gymnasts is approximately sixteen, and for elite female swimmers it is eighteen: in the light of this it is hardly surprising that coaches feel driven to exploit young talent, and to grab the attention of gifted performers at an early age, before other sports and interests interfere. Take for example Martina Hingis or Tiger Woods, athletes senior in status but certainly not in age. Another contributory factor in some sports is that they require increasingly complex movements which take a long time to develop and are best learned when children are small, light and have few perceptions about difficulty. Whatever the reason behind the search for talented youngsters, this is altogether a sensitive area, and there are key questions that must be asked: for instance, how is this process being undertaken? And how do we know if are selecting the right children to be the sporting superstars of tomorrow ?

In essence there are two areas to consider under this heading: first the identification of talent; and second the pathways that are being followed.

## What is Talent?

So what is talent, and what exactly are we looking for? This is a very complex
question: in a generic way it is predicting future success on the basis of current
performance and personal characteristics, and to begin with it involves looking
at the whole spectrum of attributes that make up the elite athlete.

### The Attributes of the Elite Athlete

1. *State of health.*   This embraces the general functioning of the body, and might
include considerations such as how often an individual succumbs to low-
level infections such as colds, and how fast he recovers. Also of concern would
be the state of the cardiac and respiratory systems in terms of effective
functioning for sports performance. The relative importance of this will vary
from one sport to another — in endurance sports for instance it will be more
critical.

2. *Physical development.*   This refers to the height and weight of the athlete, the
shape of the body and the relative proportions of the limbs; again the importance of this will vary from sport to sport. So for example in rhythmic gymnastics the ideal body shape is very slim but with long legs in relation to the rest of
the body, whereas a hammer thrower's body shape would have to be much bigger, with long arms an advantage.

Quite a lot is known about the types of physique that are successful at
elite adult level in both individual and team sports, and body typing takes
height, weight, limb girth and bone length into consideration when evaluating
to what extent performers are similar. As children are still growing this
procedure is less relevant; however, it does highlight the problem of whether
the measurements of immature bodies will give definite answers to
questions of future success, and until each sport has reliable data as to whether
juvenile size can predict final stature, and whether rates of growth can
predict who will or will not best suit a certain sport, then these
measurements are misleading.  It is more realistic to take the measurements of
a child's full height, its sitting height and its arm span say, three times a year.
This can help to map growth rate, which apart from anything else is
beneficial in that at times of peak change the coach will know to modify training loads.

Whilst this data  may suggest possible unsuitability  to certain sports as an
elite adult, it does not preclude initial involvement in those sports. Consider the
child who at nine was an excellent high jumper, but at fourteen is still the same

height: thus although early indications suggested that she might have elite potential, this was not the case.

How far a child can progress in a sport may be decided purely on the basis of physical size. Thus children who develop at an early age may become too heavy to compete later on; partners in sports acrobatics may become too disparate to be able to continue to work together; a child may become too tall to perform the more complicated movements in gymnastics, or may remain too small in stature to be able to continue to play as a goalkeeper in football. These are all illustrations of performers outgrowing an activity; however, it should not limit their future involvement in other sports. It is only fair that the parent should know this at as early an age as possible so that the child can transfer to a sport to which he or she is better suited at the most appropriate time, and when the child is still enthusiastic. Some former female gymnasts may be ideally suited to the pole vault in athletics, but they and their parents need to be aware that they can transfer. There are sports for people of all shapes and sizes, and it is merely a question of matching the child to the physical profile required by any given sport.

3. *General physical preparation.*   Here we are considering the basic physical elements that are involved in performance, namely strength, speed, flexibility, muscular endurance and stamina. Each sport will place a slightly different emphasis on the above components in order to meet its needs. Recently coaches have shown considerable interest in employing the specific tests which assess these components of fitness. However, physical fitness testing is rather a mixed blessing at this age because most tests were actually designed for adults; this makes many of them inappropriate for children, whose bodies are often less able to cope with the stresses that such tests impose. Coaches should therefore be wary of relying too much on the predictions of these types of test. On the other hand, tests of skill and co-ordination give a better indication of suitability. Where tests are used, this should be at intervals which allow for developmental and training changes to provide meaningful progress in performance. The purpose, conduct and results of the tests need to be carefully explained so that the child understands how to improve and is compared with their previous performance rather than with others.

4. *Psychological factors.*   These are critical to the elite performer, and include having good concentration and being able in stress management, also having self-confidence, mental toughness and visualization skills.

Related to this is the child's ability to learn from its environment: thus those who watch demonstrations carefully and identify those bits of information which are of importance in the successful execution of an action or movement probably a) learn with fewer repetitions, and b) have a better mental picture of what they are required to do.

The ability of the child to analyse and understand the game is an important attribute for making good early decisions. This is often refered to as anticipa-

*Talent is identified early in gymnastics.*

tion, or the ability to 'read the game'. Therefore watching sport with them — be this on television, video or live — allows conversation which can focus on what they notice about skills, and what things influence success; for instance, they will observe that the position of body parts at the start of movements will cause certain outcomes, both wanted and unwanted. Consistent performers will have good memory systems which will help them at such decision-making points; moreover, recognizing patterns of activity speeds up the best guess at what is required, and provides more time for execution. For instance getting to a loose ball as early as possible in open play in team sport allows more decision-making time and more possible options to be used.

Learning and retaining for future use aspects of skill and strategy will eventually demarcate those with potential from those with developed ability. Talks by coaches, interviews, and official texts on strategy as well as technique can all help, provided the information gleaned is in simple form and is retained. Simple memory tests related to sport can help develop this ability.

5. *Technical ability*   This relates to the technical skills of the sport, from basic foundation skills to complex skills; it also looks at skills performed in a training situation to those performed in a competitive one. This is often a consistent focus in determining the 'talent level' of a young performer.

6. *Personality factors*   Often seen to be the difference between the elite and the very good: they refer to an athlete's desire and motivation to participate, his capacity to be self-disciplined, to work hard and to endure pain and tiredness, and his desire to compete. Questioning children as to why they want to do something, and how much and how often, gives clues as to their level of drive and commitment. This will be influential in sustaining their involvement, as well as motivating them to achieve higher standards of personal performance. It also serves as a useful check to ensure that it is the child rather than the parent who wishes to continue involvement at that level and in that sport.

The mental capacity to select, control and execute movements, often under some degree of pressure and competition, will greatly influence the level to which a performer can play the game. It is somewhat surprising therefore that little attention is given to this factor, either through formal assessment or by periodic observation. It is obviously an area of great scope where simple intervention is a valid exercise.

7. *Support mechanisms*   The support factor is critical for young elite athletes, and is often the difference between success and failure. Does the young athlete have parents who will take him to training, and pay for it, take him to competitions, be there for him when it doesn't go well, but not give him added pressure to do well? This is a lot to ask from parents, and in a sense they have to be as committed as their children if excellence is to be achieved. There is no doubt that involvement in the process of nurturing young talent can be expensive and

time-consuming. The role of the parent — often the mother — of gifted children at this middle school age becomes a daily round of laundering training kit, providing energy-giving meals, transporting to training venues and providing emotional support, at the same time as having to fulfil work and household commitments, as well as trying to meet the needs of all other family members. As it may take a performer anywhere between five and seven years of concentrated involvement to aspire to levels of national recognition, the commitment needs to be long term. It therefore makes more than a subtle change to the home routine, and as such may not suit all families; and this could ultimately impinge on the progress made by the talented athlete.

Parents need to be aware of the following factors before they commit themselves and their children to elite sport:

• They will need to consider available transport, to rearrange mealtime schedules, and relinquish other time-intensive commitments.

• The scale and cost of equipment, travel requirements and time away from school may focus the mind when selecting a sport.

• Be realistic from the start. The opportunities to earn a career from sport are probably not worthy of much consideration given that less than 0.1 per cent of all sportsperformers are professional. However, this situation is starting to change with the advent of lottery funding, and many more possibilities may arise in the next millennium.

Each of these factors contributes to the make-up of the elite athlete, and will ultimately determine excellence in sports performance. So much for general traits which may suggest that some individuals are better placed initially to learn quickly in sport. This vision of generally having the right stuff has to translate into the specific selection criteria required by the governing bodies of sport. This contentious issue, seemingly wrapped in mystique and secrecy, needs to be better understood, and is the next useful port of call.

## Selecting Talented Children

In general, selection of talent focuses on the skills that children exhibit, and different sports really need to identify the attributes that they consider to be critical for success. However, many sports have failed to do this in any systematic way, and it appears that it is often those children who exhibit a greater range of skills at a younger age who are deemed to be talented. This is often the main criterion when selecting children for elite training programmes in sport, and very rarely are factors 1, 4, 6 and 7 considered.

The process of selecting children is still very subjective and limited, and it therefore comes as no surprise that the wrong children are selected, and that children with more enduring potential are overlooked. There are many examples of this, perhaps the most notable being Ian Wright who was not picked up as a young player by any of the top clubs. But how many more potential superstars are never identified because they have not been assessed in a complete way? Each sport needs to review very carefully the process of talent identification, and to consider each child in a more holistic way if true champions are to be found and developed — early flashes of skilful performance do not necessarily make the champions of the future.

We will now consider some of the ways in which talented youngsters are spotted.

## Competition Results

One of the most common routes to selection into elite training programmes in individual sports is by results, so for example a regional squad will be made up of the top twelve finishers in the regional championships. This is clearly a limited way to choose children for elite training since it is based on their performance on just one day: it does not take into account any of the other factors necessary for the development of a champion, nor is there any examination of the personal circumstances that surround the performance. As such it is also limited in its likelihood of identifying future success.

## Squad Trials

Most national governing bodies have in place some type of squad trial system for selecting regional and national squads. This is generally by invitation on the basis of previous competition results. The athletes are observed playing the sport, possibly only on one occasion, and from this they are selected for particular squads or teams. Again, the emphasis is on technical performance and physical performance.

## Scouts

Some sports — most notably pro football clubs — will employ scouts whom they trust have sufficient knowledge of the game to be able to spot the talented players of the future. Scouts will observe young players over a few matches and recommend them on the basis of their observations. Whilst this has advantages over other systems it is very subjective and does not allow for exploration of all the factors identified.

All the above systems rely on the children already being part of a sports club. In the UK there is no attempt to identify talented children who may not be participating at a reasonable level, and as a result the pool of potential talent is already diminished.

## *Talent Spotting in Australia*

In Australia there is a total commitment to participation in sport at all levels, its people firmly believing that a sporting nation is a healthy, working nation. The need to fund this centrally has been recognized, and it is part of government policy to ensure maximum participation in sport by its citizens. Such a policy means that potential talent can be spotted early, and it is helped in this by the organization 'Sport Search', which operates in the following way: all primary school children are assessed in some very basic physical tests, the assessments being initiated by specialist teachers in school. Following these the children are given a list of the top ten sports for which it is thought they will be most suited. This information is processed by a sports development officer who will monitor the children and try to align them with appropriate sports clubs. The basic theory is that there is a sport for everyone, even if it might be one that the child has little or no knowledge of. By providing these links the potential pool of talent is much bigger for the elite coaches to draw upon.

Within this system there is a second phase called 'Talent Search': this seeks to monitor and assess further the progress of the children within the scheme. It is through this system that the Australians have produced world champions in a number of sports, but notably in women's rowing.

Clearly the process of doing a few basic tests is not a watertight method of selecting talent, but it does actively involve many more children in sport. And once in the system there is a greater likelihood of talented children being spotted and nurtured.

All national governing bodies will have in place some recognized pathway for elite performers. These pathways will typically begin in schools or local clubs, and will culminate in national squads for potential international performers. The age that children will be brought into the system will vary greatly from sport to sport. So for example in gymnastics you could be in a national junior squad from the age of ten, yet children are not accepted into athletic clubs much before they are eleven.

The pathways will follow the model of 'foundation', 'participation' and 'performance to excellence'. Different sports will organize squads for talented children in different ways, and will have very different expectations in terms of training, commitment and competition.

## Training

Having selected the athlete, the following key questions need to be addressed: the amount of training to give him or her, and the amount and level of competition, and the individual's level of commitment to the sport. There seems to be a progression within sport towards the idea that more is better, but this is not necessarily the case, and very real concerns are being voiced regarding the

*A young gymnast working with her coach.*

amount of training that some athletes are regularly undertaking. There are no controls on the amount of time that children can spend training, unlike many other activities in which they can be involved. For example, there are strict controls on how long children can 'work', but none of these seem to apply to sport, and in some disciplines they are most definitely working very hard. So maybe it is appropriate to review the practices in sport that allow ten-year-olds to train up to thirty hours per week, and perhaps to ask who might be benefiting from such practices. There are many athletes who have fallen casualty to too much training at too young an age — Jennifer Capriati is a classic example of this. However, there are many more children who are victims of this but who have never become famous.

The issue here is known as 'burn-out', its main cause being too much training, to the point of physical exhaustion; very often this means that the body can never recover fully, so there is a greater probability of injury, illness and stress. Furthermore children who find themselves in this situation will almost certainly not have the psychological mechanisms to recognize what is happening to them, nor will they know how to cope, or what to do about it. Therefore great care must be taken by both coaches and parents to ensure that young athletes are not being burnt out: some never recover. When a child is selected into any training programme there needs to be a clear agreement between coach, parents and athletes as to exactly what is expected from the other parties. Thus some form of contract should be drawn up to ensure that everyone fully understands the level of commitment and the work that is going to be undertaken. Talented athletes do not occur by chance, and it is only by everyone working together that such talent can be nurtured and success achieved.

## Coach—Athlete Relationships

The truth about talented children is that they are likely to spend more and more time training — which means of course that they will be spending more and more time in the company of their coach. The quality of this relationship therefore becomes central to the psychological and physical well-being of the child, and inevitably problems of one sort or another will be encountered.

In a coach—athlete relationship where the athlete is a child or even a young teenager, the balance of power is always held by the coach; moreover it is the coach who ultimately decides whether or not the athlete has the potential to become a professional or to go to the Olympics, and the athlete knows this. It is also tacitly understood that it will be hard work to achieve success, and that possibly there is a price to pay. A recent example of this is the gymnast Dominique Moceanu who went to an American court to seek divorce from her parents because she claimed they stole her childhood. Dominique was an exceptional gymnast who at fourteen won the hearts of the American public when she took gold at the Atlanta Olympics. She now claims that her parents pushed her too hard, and only thought about gymnastics; she was quoted as saying, 'When I was young I was always in fear because I would get yelled at by my father...I never had a childhood.' She also claims that her parents have squandered her trust fund which was set up as she was still a minor in an amateur sport. Clearly this is an extreme example, but it illustrates the difficulties faced by athletes, coaches and parents to get the balance right — and in sports such as gymnastics where peaking is so early, it is even harder to achieve, given that the window of opportunity is so small.

## The Problem of Abuse

The relationship between the coach and the athlete is all-important in the development of the child into the adult. Recently there have been examples of inappropriate coaching behaviour which is clearly damaging to the children, namely sexual and physical abuse on the part of the coach, as well as emotional and psychological abuse. This type of behaviour is the exception, but nevertheless it would be naive not to acknowledge its exisistence, not to recognize that it is the responsibility of the governing bodies of sport and of the coaching fraternity to create a climate whereby the perpetrators of such behaviour are publicly exposed and prosecuted where necessary. The climate of opinion has changed and there is now a greater awareness of the issue. But coaching in sport still provides easy access to children, and the credentials of volunteer coaches have often not been checked scrupulously enough. (Ways in which parents can have peace of mind were discussed in Chapter 3.)

Another area of concern is the extent to which emotional and psychological abuse is practised. Emotional abuse is defined by the NSPCC as being 'where children are harmed by constant threats, verbal attacks, taunting or shouting', the consequences of such abuse being that a child becomes withdrawn or aggressive. Furthermore their understanding of emotions may become distorted, or they may be unable to express their emotions. Psychological abuse is slightly different, defined by Hart as 'any act which threatens the development of a positive and intact self-concept'. A child subjected to psychological abuse can feel deprived and rejected because its emotional needs are not being met by the adult. Thus its consequences can result in anxiety, agitation and depression, being withdrawn and fearful, and even being chronically ill.

So what has this got to do with coaches and young athletes? Unfortunately there are some coaches who adopt a coaching style that is indicative of either emotional or psychological abuse, and these individuals are, in fact, potentially damaging children in a very profound way — and it is all done in the so-called pursuit of excellence. The following observations are made by young, talented athletes, and are a sad reflection on coach—athlete relationships that are being exploited by the coach:

'As soon as you walked through the door you knew that you had done something wrong because he would start on at me. He'd pull a really stern face, and then he would scream at you; he would wave his arms around and scream... I didn't like it but I thought it was just something that you got used to.'

'She was just screaming at me, and the more she screamed the worse I got.'

'He belittled me. He'd make you look very small, and if you got above yourself he would put you straight down because otherwise he would not have that much control over you. So you did as he said: if he said jump, you would jump. If you got out of line he would insult you, or not talk to you, or not coach you.'

These quotes illustrate the painful experiences that young athletes can be subjected to at the hands of their coach. What is perhaps more worrying is that these coaches were all considered by their governing bodies as being successful, and capable of producing good results. More often than not the child will feel worthless and a failure, this in turn will damage its self-esteem; and if it happens often enough, psychological damage can occur. Thus the behaviour of a coach can directly influence the psychological well-being of the child.

It is also important for parents to monitor their child carefully, and to speak out if they observe any of the behaviours listed above which are indicative of problems being experienced. It is important when young children are identified as being talented that a three-way system of communication is established between the coach, parent and child.

To ensure that your child is being coached in an appropriate way the following guidelines might help:

- Do have regular meetings with the coach.
- Do discuss progress and plans for your child.
- Do watch training sessions. Question those coaching environments that never let parents in.
- Do discuss training with your child.
- Do become aware of changes in your child's behaviour.

## Summary

In conclusion, successful early performances, often in a public domain, will sow the seeds of expectation for parents and coaches. This may range from an idea that a child can enjoy and be a success in sport, to the mapping out of a professional career at a very early age. The financial trappings of such a lifestyle, and the determination of some parents to push their children towards that goal, are evident, but they are questionable. The idea that some people are naturally talented continues to be hotly disputed: theoretically it can be contended that regardless of the care with which a child has been selected, its parents will always be the most important factor in its potential success in sport. Whilst inherited potential is important in all sports, clearly providing the right environment and motivations to learn specific tasks is more influential. Whatever holds sway, it is probably more useful to consider those with so-called talent as having a number of attributes which directly influence skill-learning. Positive thinkers will see that these are the tasks which must be addressed if the pursuit of giftedness is to be realized in the face of increased competition, seeking common goals. Provided that parents and coaches are sure that this is what the child wants, the cost incurred will not be seen as a debt to be paid back by achievement at a later date.

Clearly, middle-years children experience considerable change in size, weight and functional ability. The latter can be seen by the wide range of activities and non-specific fundamental skills that they acquire during the four years from age seven. These help them to develop a broad vocabulary of movement patterns before they reach the secondary level sports experience. There appears to be little difference between the physical characteristics of boys and girls prior to the onset of puberty, and this supports the view that there is no physiological reason why the sexes cannot learn and compete equitably with each other. Specifically, boys demonstrate a slightly stronger hand grip and are better in skills which rely on stamina and speed of movement. Girls, on the other hand, exhibit better balance, co-ordination, flexibility and overall movement control. However, this parity is about to change forever as children enter the rollercoaster of puberty.

PART THREE
# THE SECONDARY YEARS

*As children develop into teenagers and young adults their participation in sport will involve more specialized training and greater opportunities for competition. It is important during these years that they receive the best possible support and guidance to enable them to progress towards fulfilling their sporting potential.*

*The key issues examined in this part are factors that may influence performance including puberty, adolescent response to exercise, development of physical fitness and advanced skill training.*

*As children move into adolescence there are greater opportunities for competing in their chosen sport. This section considers the psychological preparation for competition, team building and coping with pressure. It concludes by considering the impact of injury from a physical and psychological perspective.*

# CHAPTER SEVEN

# You're Ready For Take-Off!

## Puberty in Girls

Generally, girls enter puberty considerably before boys, and physically develop within a shorter time span. Normally puberty starts in girls between the ages of ten and twelve; the release of certain hormones leads to changes of appearance and function, which on average are completed in twenty-four to thirty months. During this time the pituitary gland's secretions stimulate the ovaries to produce oestrogen, and this leads initially either to breast budding or the emergence of pubic hair, with the start of periods approximately twelve months later. A continuing trend is that the average age of menarche, or the onset of the first period, is marginally reducing each decade — in some Scandinavian countries children are just 8.5 years when their period starts. Recent studies suggest that participation in formal training prior to puberty will consistently delay the start of the first period; thus in sports which require time-intensive sessions at an early age, such as swimming and gymnastics, for every six months before puberty that heavy training commenced, menarche is delayed for a further six months. Whilst this may worry some observers, this deceleration towards womanhood has one sport-specific advantage, in that it simultaneously delays the associated growth spurt and weight gain. This may be important in, say, gymnastics, when training involves the learning of increasingly complex routines and skills, and where a short, light performer (with a lower centre of gravity and greater power-to-weight ratio) is more likely to retain a steep learning curve. However, there is a down side to intense early involvement.

By delaying the start of regular monthly periods, the release of the growth and development hormone, oestrogen, is similarly put on hold. If this occurs in weight-conscious athletes, they may deliberately or unintentionally restrict their intake of essential nutrients, and as a result key structural elements of the body suffer; in particular, precocious bones may be prone to brittleness which, at this stage in life, can result in stress fractures. Unfortunately it appears that this may also set a related trend, namely that the individual becomes more susceptible to the adult version known as osteoporosis. Intense exercise without the hormonal release is not backed up by sufficient bone strengthening, particularly when the performance demands repeated take-offs, landings, stops, turns and restarts. Dietary checks linked to training regulation with some consideration of preventative prophylactic supports at this key developmental stage can help.

Increasing hip width, leg length and torso breadth account for an upward weight shift, and are associated with proportional limb growth. Whilst flexibility potential is retained, running stride length and efficiency can decrease somewhat if the athlete doesn't relearn and practise this skill. In girls, shoulder and torso width consistency and elbow movement anomalies maintain, rather than develop, their throwing and carrying abilities.

As a guide, girls can be expected to grow steadily during the two and a half years from the age of ten and a half. During that time their yearly change in height can exceed 7–9cm (3–.75in) at its peak. Whilst the timing differs from one girl to another, two patterns remain consistent: firstly, that girls become women at a time when boys are merely nearer to becoming men; and that the shortened female growth spurt ultimately accounts for the average height difference of 10–15cm (4–6in) between fully developed males and females.

During this time, girls can be expected to gain slightly more fat mass than lean body mass as compared to boys who have also completed their growing years: at the age of sixteen, studies suggest that girls have, on average, almost twice the body fat percentage of similarly aged boys. With regular aerobic exercise this may be kept in check, if it is a problem; however, it may also help to account for the amazing performances of long distance swimmers, who often manage to maintain an appropriate body temperature in cold oceanic waters for many hours.

## Puberty in Boys

Boys also undergo significant physical changes as they leave childhood and enter adolescence. They lag approximately 18–24 months behind girls, and this continues for as long again after most girls have completed the process. This means that they are physically immature for longer and are able to adapt to their changing bodies more slowly because of the extended nature of their structural transition. This longer time period allows both greater final growth, and greater rate of change relative to girls.

Structurally, the accelerated growth of the male sex organs appears before the development of pubic hair. Facial hair similarly precedes the deepening of the voice, penile enlargement and mature sexual functioning. Because of the developmental nature of these changes boys will appear to vary greatly when compared for physical maturity between the ages of twelve and fifteen. For boys this can be a sensitive issue, and it should be explained to them that this staggered change is natural and that it cannot be influenced; otherwise they will tend to make negative self-perceptions and to draw unfortunate and probably inaccurate comparisons. Each boy's natural body clock will determine at what point the change will be initiated.

The most important consequence of these changes for boys is the increased performance potential that the hormonal release of testosterone enables. Structurally the ever-widening shoulders, deepening chest and consolidation of leg length and girth reflect increasing bone growth and continuing hardening, or ossification, of the shaft of the long bones. In terms of limb function, bone development is now accompanied by changes in the cross-sectional area of muscle. Potentially boys will be able to develop significantly greater throwing, hitting and kicking force as well as starting speed, acceleration, and the ability to maintain speed over longer distances. Whilst some of this potential will start to develop purely because of changes associated with growth and normal physical activity, it also becomes more linked to the quality and quantity of work undertaken, and associated factors such as nutrition. Therefore it is towards the completion of this process, in both boys and girls alike, that the selection of developmentally related activity and conditioning becomes crucial.

As mentioned previously boys grow later, for longer, and often more quickly than most girls. Growth experts suggest that they can be expected to gain between 10 and 30cm (4–12in) in the thirty months to their fifteenth birthday. Their peak growth rate is slightly more than that of girls, and it often occurs more than two years after girls have reached the same point. Weight gain is directly related to structural changes, and so it is not surprising that they can put on more than a third of their current weight again during this time. The composition and distribution of this increase contrasts with the female pattern in that the testosterone-based changes create a heavier, more sculptured upper body with less hip change. Boys do not gain so much fat mass as girls at this stage, and their bones can become more dense as a positive result of appropriate exercise involvement.

So early teenagers now look and appear much more like the adults they hope to emulate — but if they have sporting interests, it is important to see these changes for what they are. Being bigger and heavier may suggest better physical potential, but physical changes tend to precede emotional maturity, physical co-ordination and the social skills also associated with games and activities. Therefore it is probably wise to investigate which forms of exercise are now worth introducing in view of what we know about the pattern of their training adaptation and improvement.

Exactly how young bodies cope and respond to the more adult exercise regimes which start to feature at this age becomes fundamental to selecting sports training programmes.

## Tackling Adult Training Regimes

In the past, sport seems to have lagged a long way behind education, childcare and many of the creative arts in considering children's abilities and needs when learning new activities. For too long enthusiastic youngsters laboured under the needless burden of minimally adapted playing areas, equipment, time periods and rules which were more often a test of their young age or immature development, than a test of skill. This highlighted their shortcomings rather than their abilities, and probably led to many of them looking for other activities which gave them more of a chance of success. Thankfully within the last twelve years or so that has all changed for the better, largely because of an intensive study of children's response to activity and exercise. Their response to exercise is particularly noteworthy here.

Very often children are experiencing a considerable amount of change at the same time as they are being introduced to sports which are more equally reliant on skill and fitness than was previously the case. They notice that some of their group or classmates have grown and matured a lot in often a short period of time whilst others have not. The associated level of ability is therefore wider at a time of increasing challenge, and when the notion of formal training is first introduced as a, rather than the, means of improvement. This alludes to the fact that unlike their adult counterparts, with children it is impossible to attribute positive change in performance solely to growth, or to maturity of the developing system, or to structured activity. Therefore the only sensible course of action is to ensure that the synthesis between these areas is retained. There are too many stories of children pushed too hard in training at too early an age to suggest that they cope well with the imposition of adult training loads.

• Parents need to ask questions about training loads, and coaches need to monitor carefully the amount of work in sessions and the total involvement for the week.

• Diaries or logs of training activity are not only good motivational tools, they are vital to ensure that workloads remain related to improvement, and to point up the warning signs of overtraining, overuse injury, staleness and performer burnout.

## The Problems of Aerobic Training for Children

So if we accept the general warning about children enjoying childhood for its own sake before they opt for a greater degree of involvement towards a more adult standard, what do we know about their abilities?

Whilst stamina, or aerobic endurance, is vital for the longevity of the cardio-respiratory system and almost equally important for participation and recovery, the type of training involved is often problematic for children. Firstly, logic tells us that there must be a link with the rise in greenhouse gasses, the levels of specific pollution, and the increased incidence of environmentally related asthma. At present it is estimated that this affects one child in seven in this country, and that it is gaining. This can make the thought of doing continuous whole body activity for a sustained time period at best difficult, or at worst unthinkable on the increasing number of warm days that we appear to have.

Studies show that when undertaking aerobic tasks, children have to work harder at an earlier stage in the exercise than adults. Interestingly this does not appear to affect their perception of how hard the work is, even though the physical effort required to sustain the level of performance is very real. A sensible way to build exercise tolerance would be to organize shorter bouts of activities on days when the environment does not interfere too much. In physical education lessons in the past the accepted policy was only to run on days when the weather had ruled out normal activities; however, in the light of these more recent findings this can have done nothing whatsoever to foster a lifetime's enjoyment of this activity.

Tests of aerobic ability are often related to an adult's norms, a practice which implies that adults and children cope with progressively harder aerobic work in the same way. Research has shown this to be untrue, however, in that children get to a point where the lactate by-product of the exercise adversely affects their performance in half the time that it would an adult's. Therefore the coach or teacher needs to ensure that they do not drive young performers into continuing beyond the levels of prior agreement. It may be that by improving the technical skills required for such tests, and by teaching pace judgement, opportunities for improvement will be maximized anyway

## Post-Puberty

Although girls and boys appear to compare equally favourably before puberty, they differ noticeably from that point onwards. The early growth spurt for girls corresponds to an initial advantage in terms of aerobic ability until the age of thirteen to fourteen. Thereafter their increased bodyweight, smaller lung capacity and the change in their leg action appear to prevent their aerobic abilities from developing and improving naturally. The ultra-distance, marathon and triathlon records for women seem to be consistently lowered as they approach male standards; nevertheless, the effect of appropriate training on all three variables can greatly increase ability.

Boys catch up and pass girls in terms of both aerobic capacity and power. This encompasses the total energy which is available to perform sustained, progressive work, and is often measured by a maximal oxygen uptake test. It appears that it is most beneficial to introduce aerobic work at a time corresponding to peak change in height.

### Running Skills

Children cope better with sub-maximal, rather than maximal work, and are well equipped to maintain running speed with training. It would appear that steady running which progresses gradually in intensity but maintains volume, or vice versa, provides a useful training regime with predictable improvement. Running should be conducted at a pace at which talking is still possible, and initially on flat surfaces, and it should take place at times when energy levels are high and children are clear of infections which may affect respiration. They will cope better with gradually increasing distance or variable terrain than increased pace at an early age. However, the need to learn pace is still an important running-related skill, and one which can be introduced at this time. Using a known course with permanent markers and a stopwatch, coaches can teach children how to start at the right speed so they do not fatigue too quickly. By dividing the remainder of the run into equal time intervals they soon develop the ability to judge accurately how fast to go to maintain speed. This will eventually allow them to perform unsupervised runs at the appropriate pace as required in a warm-up. This can be gradually extended in distance to improve the fitness effect.

## The Warm-Up

This whole body requirement is also a must before stretching work which is the practical means by which muscles are prepared for exercise. Before children reach puberty, the warm-up can be more fun-oriented, with movements which stress control, directional variation and co-ordination; moreover at this stage boys and girls are similar in so far as their need for skill development is greater than their need to maintain or improve flexibility. Whilst girls are slightly more flexible than boys, the difference is much smaller than it is likely to be in the teenage years and beyond. The middle years' child appears to have as much flexibility as it generally requires unless it is directly involved in sports such as gymnastics, where trainability effects have been noted. After the age of thirteen it is noticeable that where the male range of movement is reduced — and we will return to the reasons why this happens when we consider strength development — a girl's structural capabilities are by contrast increased. For instance the hip or pelvis is lighter and smoother in girls, and this prevents some of the loss of mobility which in particular seems to disadvantage some male football and rugby players. The central recess of the pelvis is also larger in girls, though evidently this is for non-sporting reasons, namely in preparation for childbirth.

As a rule of thumb, before young adolescents commence exercise they should spend twice as long on stretching as they do on their initial running: therefore five minutes of lightly accelerating running will raise the body temperature sufficiently and this should be followed by ten minutes of stretching. At this point the emphasis is on controlled movements into held positions which to begin with are not too ambitious. The performer should try to hold stretches for a period of 10–12 seconds so that the body's natural defence mechanisms relax enough to allow muscles to extend on the basis that they are warm, stable and gently lengthened. Starting with the head and working down the body ensures that no important groups are omitted. The muscles which control and support the hips and shoulders are worthy of special attention, as is the back which links the two. Stretches which hold positions can be followed by slow movements which mimic the range required in sport-specific situations. This can be particularly useful when working outside on cold days, where the effect of raising the body temperature in the run is soon lost because of the more static nature of stretching.

## The Peak Growth Years

When girls and boys are at their peak growth years (14.5 and 17 years respectively) they may commence training in sports which require extended ranges of movement. Greater flexibility is an advantage in sports where power is important, such as in striking an object, pulling a throwing implement or propelling the body forwards. Warm-up alone will merely maintain the prevailing range of ability, and a separate session may be needed when the core body temperature is much warmer (i.e. after 30 minutes of gradually extended whole body exercise, stretching and further movement) but before the fatigue or co-ordination losses occur. The sole purpose of these sessions — often conducted indoors in a warm environment with simple gymnasium equipment available — is to undertake a relatively small number of stretching exercises for an extending period of time.

Research suggests that merely holding a position for between 20 and 90 seconds will have a positive and indeed permanent effect on muscle length. It can also create some residual soreness so would need to be introduced carefully and under supervision. Towels, dynabands, wallbars, benches and door frames can all be adapted so that passive exercises can be performed. In this variation, for more mature performers who have some degree of control and responsibility, the performer uses a form of leverage to attain more movement in the end position than was previously the case. Athletes should be encouraged to learn how to reduce muscular tension by controlling and listening to their breathing; this skill should be well developed before more advanced forms of stretching such as Proprioceptive Neuromuscular Facilitation (PNF) are considered during late adolescence.

## Improving the Body's Output

Losing flexibility in spite of more time spent effectively warming up is a frustrating sequel to regular involvement in training programmes. It appears to be related to the fact that as we get towards the end of fatiguing training, in most sports our range of movement is reduced. The one activity which surprisingly is the exception to the rule is strength training. This involves the athlete working against some form of resistance, natural or otherwise, in a way which encourages the body eventually to adapt, and to demonstrate an improved working capacity as a result. If a cycle of work against a slightly heavier load can be followed by rest and recovery, supplemented with balanced nutritional provision, the body can progressively improve its output. This initially will lead to greater movement efficiency, and if repeated for a period of time in excess of four weeks, to changes in actual muscular strength. This may in turn improve how much force is produced and the ease with which movements can be accomplished. However, it is subject to an initial 'settling-in' period where it is likely that the new training programme may have a temporarily negative effect on sport performance. A month of two appropriate workouts a week will lead to structural changes within the muscle long before there is any noticeable change in size for boys or tone for girls.

## Resistance Work

As girls complete puberty first, they are ready before boys to benefit from the trainable effects of resistance work. It is recommended that to begin with they work to gain greater muscular control over their bodies by learning simple circuit training-type exercises, but working against their bodyweight rather than against any external load. Once technique has improved and they can work for between 20 and 40 seconds at a continuous pace, they may be ready for more all-action activities (with monitored work and rest periods). The need to develop local muscular conditioning and to reduce naturally developing body fat suggests that aerobic dance, aquarobics and circuit training should be considered next. To help their motivation, girls should start to keep regular training diaries so they can see how their loading, ability to recover and total amount of work done are improving. Whilst there may be some exercises that boys do better than girls — particularly those which develop upper body strength — otherwise there are no other differences in the expectations of work amounts, intensities or recoveries. Quite simply girls can work and recover at the same rate as boys if they train regularly.

## Exercising With Weights

The same principles would apply when from fifteen to sixteen — exactly when depends on their maturity and bone development — girls start to exercise with weights. The dominance of oestrogen, compared with much lower levels of testosterone in girls, causes exercised muscle to define itself more clearly or to tone up. Three sets of twelve repetitions of the upper and mid-sections, and leg work amounting to ten to twelve exercise stations will promote muscle integrity rather than size development, with fat loss a related benefit. A total session time of thirty minutes and upwards will further mobilize these unwanted stores as a source of continued energy. Work should be slow on the recovery or return phase of the exercise and more active on the positive, against resistance effort. All movements conducted through the fullest range of movement will not only strengthen the relatively weak start and finish of range sections, but will enhance passive flexibility at the same time.

Boys following a similar, if later starting programme will also learn essential body stabilization before attempting to utilize their greater potential for strength and size increases. In circuit training their arms and legs sometimes develop at the expense of the generally weaker mid-section; therefore stomach, back and side trunk exercises should be stressed, along with opportunities to improve groin, back and hamstring flexibility during the recovery between exercises. Muscle gain can sometimes coincide with flexibility loss in boys so it is important that both are developed in tandem. Once they can handle two sessions a week, with one emphasizing endurance and the other strength, with good form and full working ranges, weight training can be started.

Large muscle group exercises should precede the more easily fatigued areas such as the calf and hip flexors, and body parts should be worked in rotation initially to allow local recovery between exercises designed to develop the same areas. Exercises where the weight is held or lifted by the hands are also better suited to the beginner than those which load the spine or involve trunk rotation. Other sound principles would include ensuring that both the dominant and non-dominant sides of the body are equally developed, as well as selecting exercises which develop the front and back equally (front exercises are generally those with a pushing action, whilst ones which pull work the upper spine).

**Machine and Free Weight Exercises**
Boys and girls should be introduced to both machine and free weight exercises because these balance the overall programme. Machines are safer in that they only require the new performer to work in one direction, and if control is lost during the movement, the weight will return to the performer without causing injury. The gymnasium supervisor, on the other hand, may be less happy if this occurs and is likely to suggest that too heavy a weight has been attempted. This highlights one of the disadvantages of such systems (multi-station, integrated units) in that they tend to work mainly the dominant or prime muscle group responsible for the movement involved.

Most sports require performers to be balanced when executing skills, and so free weights are more relevant once rudimentary control has been established. They also allow movements to be modified, and so late adolescents can practise movement routines in sport as they start to train more specifically. Enlisting the help of a specialist weights coach can assist with this when the time comes. Similarly, once strength starts to be developed, it makes sense to consider a related performance factor: speed.

## Speed Improvement

In the skill-hungry years between seven and eleven, children are well motivated to learn and demonstrate new capabilities. Some of these require elements of body control and limb manipulation which need learning and practice together. It is probably useful that they do not also have to cope with training to become quicker, stronger or more flexible at the same time. Whilst all three can be practised during the middle years, the amount of improvement is very limited — so much so that they are better left until after peak growth in adolescence, when they are more trainable. This means that practice brings greater improvement provided the level of intensity and the duration of concentrated work is appropriate to children's capabilities. Speed is equally poor in pre-adolescent girls and boys, probably because long-legged children have to stabilize their foot control for starting and turning before they can increase their rate of change or cadence.

After the age of fourteen it is worth spending time on speed improvement. In most leg-dominant sports, performers have to start, accelerate, maintain speed and change direction with predictable regularity. Children's reaction times — that is, the time taken to respond to some type of stimuli such as a command, movement or whistle — improve steadily throughout adolescence, as does their mental preparedness to be ready to move, albeit to a lesser extent without specific training. They can be taught how to place the feet effectively to get the most out of an explosive start, provided they work over short distances and the recovery period is age related. Specific foot speed drills isolate individual elements of the running cycle and teach concentration skills. Runs over short distances, where athletes go up a gear every 10m in a total distance of not more than 40m, introduce the consideration of how to beat someone and stay ahead of them if both are moving. Once these have been mastered individually, practice with team-mates can allow relative comparison, provided the emphasis is put on judging improvement from trial to trial, rather than person to person.

### Agility Work

Agility work forms a natural link between speed and strength throughout the growth period. Boys' and girls' ability will be similar in that both will ebb and flow as control is gained and lost successively because of temporary co-ordination changes. Being confident when running forwards at speed allows more challenging elements to be introduced — for instance, swerving off line and returning under control, and off either foot, is integral to netball and hockey; similarly, tracking an opponent with sideways stepping, and preventing an attacking run by efficient backward speed, are both linked with football and rugby success. Again they can be improved by progressive practice which links speed with decision-making and judgement of time and space. For seventeen-year-olds and upwards these activities can be useful in the few days immediately before a competition; skipping, running drills and stair-running promote similar effects but have the legacy of greater fatigue so are better scheduled away from matches, perhaps in the earlier part of the week.

## The Advantage of Physical Training

There is no doubt that young adolescent boys and girls need the impetus of physical conditioning. During puberty, rapid bone growth overtakes the natural increase in muscle size at a time when children need greater strength, power and speed in their movements. The dual effect of exposure to mature training and the natural development from the growth spurt ensures that increasing stature is matched by physique and functional control. However, most children will see these new activities as a means to be more skilful in competitions so it is maybe worthwhile to consider the all-important link between the two at this point.

*A young elite gymnast demonstrates excellent control and strength.*

## Learning to Make Decisions

Other forms of training should integrate technical skills with decision making and physical fitness where possible. Children develop as better decision makers once they are more in control of the skill, and with guidance as to what to look for in their quest to make a quick and accurate selection in any given situation. From the age of approximately fourteen they understand the concept of abstract thought, they have developing memory systems, and they are physically better equipped to react than they were two years previously. However, their limited experience can make them either cautious or reckless in that they are still learning to make best use of the visual and verbal information they are receiving. Watching movements so that they better appreciate what signals might indicate particularly important reactions in their opponents is most beneficial from this age onwards.

Coaches can ask pertinent questions to find out if children are developing their powers of insight as a result of knowing what to look at and for how long. They need to integrate this live action which is quickly unfolding whilst rapidly searching for memories of similar experiences; this allows them to 'guesstimate' what is likely to be the best response prior to initiating an action previously trained in isolation. As a result the coach needs to refrain from immediately telling them how they did, but instead should ask them to evaluate the degree of success achieved in the preparation for, and execution of, a physical response. This will help to make them more comfortable when they are on their own, as often happens in a competitive situation.

## Increasing the Challenge

The performance of the skills themselves also needs to become more challenging at this stage. Studies have consistently found that performers who practise under varied conditions are more likely to be able to cope better under the novel conditions associated with competition (as has previously been discussed). Therefore practices which specifically mimic the situations which might be expected in the course of a competitive season provide a number of benefits: first, they can boost player confidence, or at least be a focus for reducing pre-match anxiety, as well as ensuring that players develop a problem-solving approach. This is vital if they are to make judgements consistent with those that their coach would make, at times when he or she cannot be present. Furthermore, independence of thought can be a useful self-motivator as it boosts personal control in situations where it is all too easy to feel that you are losing it. However, the physical practice of skills will also require more training, to ensure that the execution of those skills does not break down under pressure.

## Overlearning a Skill

Once an important skill has been well learned it must become a permanent feature of a performer's physical vocabulary. The old adage 'If you do not use it you will lose it' applies especially to newly learned or developed skills. It is now a case of ensuring that they are recorded or 'grooved in' by something called 'overlearning'. This is the continued practice of a learned skill to the point that its characteristics become stored in the memory structures associated with retention. This may be because the skill is particularly important, such as the quality of the first touch on the ball in hockey or football, or because a bad habit needed to be ironed out for progression to the next level. Unfortunately repetitive practice of something you can already do can induce boredom, and prevent you achieving your goal of enhanced ability. Emphasis on varied practice, performer evaluation and the maintenance of performance norms, such as setting a score out of ten for the quality of the movement as well as rating the final outcome, can help.

Essentially purposeful and more demanding practice is vital for continued application and progress during the mid- to late adolescent years. This is not always easy for the performer to handle, for two reasons. Firstly the hormonal changes largely associated with physical growth also appear to affect adversely young people's levels of patience and frustration. It also presents problems when dealing with figures in authority for a period of time, particularly for boys. The extent to which this normally occurring phenomenon interferes depends on the supportiveness of parents and coaches as well as the degree of self-awareness which develops. Secondly the coach may know that, in the long term, improvement in sport is directly related to the level of skill learning and the extent to which it can be reproduced when the heat is on. The reasons for this attention to detail and the seemingly repetitive nature of some training elements may be less clear from the performers' point of view. However, this change in perspective may be assisted by a greater understanding of the notion of competition; this will be considered next.

# CHAPTER EIGHT

# Psyched For Success

Persuading adolescents to continue to participate in sport is a big challenge for coaches and physical educators. Basically, if the sporting environment itself is challenging, fun and exciting, teenagers will stick with it; if it is not, then the lure of other activities will prevail, and not all of these are beneficial to the health and well-being of young people. Because of this, and as we become increasingly aware of the risks of sedentary living, it is crucial that sport is able to maintain their interest.

This chapter will investigate a number of different areas which have been shown to be important in the development of teenage athletes. It is important to bear in mind that the athletes in this particular age group take part in their chosen sport for extremely diverse reasons — it may include gymnasts who are already elite international athletes; those who are just beginning their participation in the sport, as in athletics; those who are involved in competitive sports; some may be involved for social reasons, and others to maintain health. Consequently each aspect of sport that we address here will inevitably be more relevant to one group than another; however, they all contribute to a coach's knowledge and understanding, and in the long term this will ultimately contribute to the development of sports at all levels in this country.

## Developing A Team

The concept of the team and all that it encompasses is one that is fundamental to sport — indeed it is a long-held conviction that through participation in team sports a child can develop leadership skills, understanding of other people and communication skills, to name but a few. It is surely significant that participation in team games at school was made compulsory by the last government, emphasizing the belief held by many that sport will have a crucial role to play in the development of the next generation of responsible citizens. So the next question is, how to develop an effective team.

### Defining 'Team'

Most people when thinking of a team will focus on those sports which involve more than one person, for example a football team or a netball team. They will also probably think of it as just the players on the pitch, but in fact this is a very narrow definition and disregards many other people who are also an essential part of its performance: the coaches, the manager, the physio, the sports scientist, to name a few — all of these contribute to a team's success. Moreover, even in individual sports one might contend that it is a 'team' working together even if this team consists of just one athlete and their coach. In their research on human functioning, psychologists refer to 'group process and dynamics', and define a group as being two or more people. We feel that it is appropriate here to adopt the same approach and consider that a 'team' is two or more people working towards common goals.

## How a Team Operates

Understanding how a team operates is crucial to the developing of better relationships between its members, and ultimately to the achieving of better performances. There has been a significant amount of research into this area, most notably by A.Carron, who has developed some excellent models to try and help us understand the complex processes that are involved in team dynamics. One of the most important concepts that has emerged from his investigations is that of team cohesion. This is a measure of how well the members of a team function together: the better they operate, the greater the team cohesion, and in fact Carron (1982) further differentiates cohesion into 'task cohesion' — how

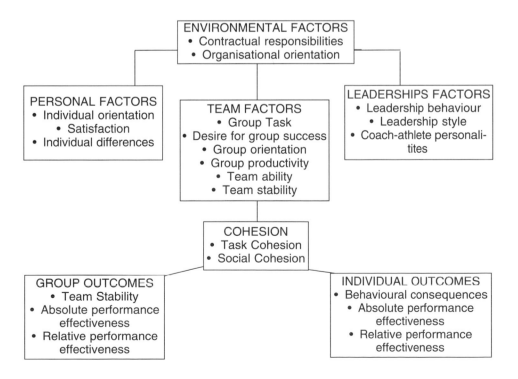

successfully team members work together to achieve team goals and objectives — and 'social cohesion', or how well the team interacts socially.

The model above highlights several key factors which contribute to the way in which a team functions, and appreciating these should help us to adopt a systematic approach to understanding cohesion in sport teams. Once an understanding has been gained, then the coach is in a position to do something about it. According to the model there are four key antecedents that will affect the team's social and task cohesion, namely environmental factors, and personal, team and leadership factors.

## The Environmental Factors

This refers to the basis on which the athletes are part of the team. So for example one player on a football team might have a different contract to another, or maybe the team members are there because they pay a subscription to a club, or because they have been selected to represent their region; moreover there are clearly umpteen different types of 'contract' that define an athlete's obligations to the team. Another 'environmental factor' is the way in which the team is organized: thus some teams compete at the highest levels and for vast sums of money, whereas at the other end of the scale there are teams who use competition as nothing more than a means of social interaction.

## The Personal Factors

This refers to the fact that a team is essentially a group of individuals, all of whom will bring their own personal 'baggage' into the team arena: this embraces socio-cultural background, ethnic origin, sex, and personal motivation. The latter determines what an individual wants from the sport — thus some people will be very task-motivated and will enjoy working hard towards team performance goals, whilst others are socially motivated and simply enjoy the interaction that is a consequence of being a member of a sports team.

## The Leadership Factors

These relate directly to the coach, specifically the way in which he (or she) behaves during training sessions and competitions. Moreover the type of leadership style that is adopted — be it democratic, autocratic or laissez-faire — will also have a direct influence on the cohesion of any team. And obviously the coach—athlete interaction is all-important: basically if they are compatible there is a stronger basis for cohesion and harmony than if there is conflict between them.

## The Team Factors

This is the team's identity, and refers to the past experiences that have been shared, also the collective desire for success, and the 'team spirit'. It also embraces the team's stability, something which can have a considerable influence on its cohesion.

Research into the relationship between cohesion — and particularly task cohesion — and performance success implies that the more interactive a team is, the better team cohesion becomes. Furthermore, those that exhibit high group cohesion have lower levels of anxiety and increased levels of self-confidence, both of which are desirable attributes to have in any team. Thus the cohesive team can be seen as providing a supportive, nurturing environment which will fulfil many emotional as well as performance needs for the young athlete. There is also strong evidence to suggest that high levels of cohesion are associated with lower drop-out rates; and since at present the attrition rate from sport is at an all-time high, especially amongst girls, it can only be useful to develop strategies that will encourage cohesion.

## Team Building

Whilst the above helps us to understand the factors involved in team cohesion, it does not tell us exactly how we can develop it. This process is commonly known as 'team building', and the coach is all-important in its achievement. Many great coaches have preached the virtues of team unity as selfless behaviour and total commitment to the team outcome. As the famous US basketball coach John Wooden said, 'It is amazing how much can be accomplished if no one cares who gets the credit!' So how is this achieved? Effective team building requires that each and every member of the team is valued for the role that they play, and its contribution to performance success. Whether yours is an elite basketball team winning major league titles or the under tens judo squad, it should be characterized by an inexorable feeling of unity between all the members, of togetherness yet of being individually valued too.

Here are some practical ways in which this can be achieved:

• Ensure that everyone on the team is valued and feels that they have an important role to play; this applies in equal measure to the most talented athletes and to the reserves. Give all members of the team praise and positive feedback for the contribution that they make. Remember that a team does not function well with people who do not feel valued.

• Know everyone on your team. Take time to invest in them as people, rather than just as players on the team: you will be richly rewarded. This can be done very simply by asking the children how things are going outside training, and making them feel that you are interested in them. Show them that you care what is happening in their lives.

• Clearly identify all the team roles and explain how they each contribute to the functioning and success of the team. Members need to know exactly what is expected of them and how they can fulfil their role. This is especially important for players who do not always get to play, because if they perceive themselves as being unimportant to the team they will often become demotivated and their self-esteem can suffer.

• Develop a team identity and a team culture. This is easily achieved with, for example, team T-shirts and tracksuits, and by organizing social activities away from training. It is also important to use team meetings effectively: first, be quite clear as to the purpose and nature of the meeting — some are to discuss issues of concern, others might be more factual. Identify the agenda well in advance, and decide how you are going to handle the ensuing proceedings. Encourage players to share their thoughts and observations on their own performance: they will often provide a valuable insight into their view of events. Do not allow a meeting to degenerate into petty criticism and backbiting: this will quickly lead to conflict and a breakdown in team cohesion. Where there are more than six people at a meeting it is generally very productive if they divide into smaller groups of two or three to discuss the issues on hand; all members then have a chance to contribute their say — in a large group, those members who are less confident might feel too intimidated to offer anything, and so will remain silent. Also, the fact that a member knows he will be listened to will help his feeling of being valued. Furthermore, even though your members might be children, don't underestimate their ability to take part in this process: they will do so more effectively than ever you might imagine, besides which it will help them develop into responsible adults.

• It is up to you to take responsibility for the team's less successful performances, so do not blame the athletes when mistakes are made: by sharing the blame they will be better able to rationalize how things went wrong, and no one will be made to feel isolated. In the same way, encourage individuals to take responsibility for their own actions: if this all happens in a supportive atmosphere the potential for them to learn, and to improve their performance is greatly increased.

• Develop clear and concise team goals, within the capabilities of all team members, and ones which they agree with.(See Chapter 5 for a full explanation on goal setting.)

• Be ready to recognize and reward excellence whenever it occurs: this can be in performance, or in attitude, or in team spirit. Make these rewards public and important to your athletes.

• Encourage members of the team to be supportive of one another, even if that might appear to conflict with personal interest. So for example a reserve player can be supportive of the player who is playing in her position, even though that player will have effectively denied her a game.

• Encourage all team members to talk to each other: they should appreciate each other's needs in the same way that you, as the coach, appreciate theirs. I remember a team meeting I had with the national team just before they competed at a World Championship: I asked how each member liked to prepare before competing, and it transpired that one athlete liked to be left completely alone. His team-mates were not aware of this, however, and had always chatted away merrily to him, giving him what they thought was encouragement, and not appreciating that this was in fact preventing him prepare properly. He had always felt that he couldn't complain because he knew they did it with the best of intentions. Clearly in this situation the team performance might well have suffered, because this member had not been able to present himself well prepared for the competition. To summarize: greater understanding and knowledge regarding individual needs within any team will help it function more effectively.

If you try to develop these aspects within your coaching sessions you will see a positive change in the functioning of the group which will benefit all members.

## Understanding Competition

So you have your team working well together in training, and the personal relationships within the team are strong — but when you go out into a competition situation some of the players always seem to perform below what you and they know they are capable of. 'What's going on'? you ask yourself.

What your athletes could be experiencing is competitive anxiety, and it will nearly always have a directly adverse effect on their performance. We will investigate this phenomenon, but before we do so we need to explore the nature of competition itself.

What is it about competition that causes young athletes to experience problems? Essentially there are three aspects of competition that place difficult demands on them: firstly, the performance is public, so everyone will see who came last in a race, or who missed the penalty kick. Secondly, in some sports the performance is evaluated down to a numerical value, so that one might be considered to be worth 8.7, and another 9.3. Thirdly there are the expectations that are imposed upon athletes by coaches, parents and team-mates.

Together these aspects comprise a powerful mixture and can change significantly how athletes think, behave and of course perform — which explains why it is difficult for them to perform to high levels of excellence in competition, even if they can do so in training. However, they can learn how to cope with competitive anxiety, in much the same way that they can be taught any other aspect of sport — but first let us try to understand the theory in order to be effective in this.

## Competitive Anxiety

Anxiety has both state and trait components. Some people have high levels of trait anxiety and will therefore be more likely to display symptoms of anxiety than those having low trait anxiety. The 'state' component refers to the fact that individuals will find that some situations produce an anxiety response, whereas others do not. So for some people the thought of talking in front of a large group of people is very distressing, whereas to someone else it is easy. On the whole, when an individual feels in control of a situation his anxiety response will be lower than when the circumstances are very unfamiliar or where he feels overwhelmed.

Current thinking regards anxiety as being multidimensional. This means that there are several components that constitute anxiety, namely cognitive anxiety, somatic anxiety and self-confidence; these interact to influence sporting performance, but they affect performance in different ways — so a closer examination of each of these is appropriate.

## Cognitive Anxiety

This refers to psychological processes which are generally viewed as being negative and detrimental to performance. These are:

- Worry
- Negative thoughts
- Feeling as if you can't cope
- Feeling confused
- Being distracted
- Inability to concentrate
- Over-narrowing of attention
- Negative images
- Feeling out of control
- Feeling scared

Research indicates that there is an inverse relationship between cognitive anxiety and performance: consequently the greater the amount of cognitive anxiety an individual is experiencing, the more it will damage his performance. There is also a temporal patterning to cognitive anxiety, indicating that an individual can be experiencing the symptoms long before a competition. Furthermore the more importance that an athlete places on a competition, the earlier the onset of cognitive anxiety. This is something that coaches need to be aware of. I have often heard coaches chastise their athletes in the days leading up to a major competition for 'not trying' or 'not concentrating'. However, by doing this they are effectively increasing the feelings of anxiety and apprehension experienced by the athlete, and this is a recipe for disaster.

## Somatic Anxiety

This refers to the physiological component of anxiety and includes the following symptoms:

- Increased heart rate
- Increased blood pressure
- Increased adrenalin
- Increased sweating
- Increased desire for urination
- Dry mouth
- Butterflies
- Increased muscle tension
- Increased blood sugar
- Increased respiration

Different athletes will experience somatic anxiety in very different ways, and clearly not all the above symptoms are detrimental to performance — in fact they may be positively crucial to some sports. However, as with many things related to anxiety, it is the interpretation of these symptoms that is important in determining whether they become detrimental or not. I remember asking a very young athlete about what she was feeling just before her first competition: she told me that she didn't have butterflies in her stomach, but wasps! Evidently this was a serious state of affairs — and what exactly were these wasps doing in her stomach anyway? We talked about it, and decided that the wasps were there to help her: by buzzing around they were giving her the extra energy that she needed to perform really well, which of course she did.

Somatic anxiety tends to increase just prior to competition — often arrival at the competition venue will trigger off its symptoms. However, it must be remembered that athletes will all differ in both the temporal patterning of somatic anxiety and the exact form it takes.

## Self-Confidence

The more self-confidence an athlete has, the better he will be able to perform. Some people believe that this is the single most critical factor in the psychological armoury of the competitive athlete, and that it is imperative that coaches focus their attention on developing this aspect of performance above all else. So what is it? In essence it is the belief in oneself to perform a desired task, and preparation prior to competition is all-important in determining how confident

*A young basketball player shows signs of worry before her forthcoming competition.*

an athlete feels. Self-confidence affects behaviour in the following ways:

- It makes us feel good and experience positive emotions
- It makes us better able to focus on the job at hand
- It allows us to take risks
- It increases how hard we work
- It increases our perseverance even when the going gets tough

It is important to remember that only some succeed because they are destined to, but most succeed because they are determined to. Conversely, self-doubt will undermine performance (examples of self-doubt will be found in the list of symptoms of cognitive anxiety) — indeed, lack of self-belief will always be the downfall of any athlete at whatever level they are competing. Let us examine the characteristics of self-confidence in order to understand it better. A critical theory has been presented by Bandura, and this provides us with a model which is referred to as 'Bandura's Self-Efficacy Theory' ('self-efficacy' is situationally specific self-confidence — so for example I might have high self-efficacy for swimming, but low for scuba diving).

According to Bandura's model there are four sources from which we derive self-confidence: performance accomplishments; modelling; verbal persuasion; and emotional arousal. These are critical to any coaching situation in that we can manipulate them to enhance the confidence of the athletes with whom we are working.

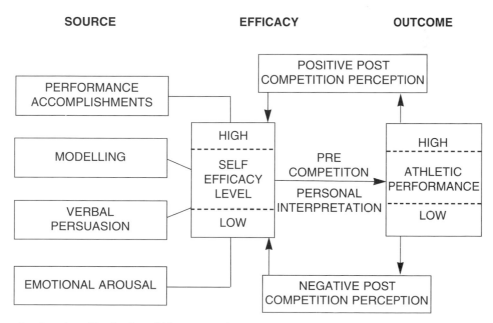

*An adaptation of Bandura's model by Gervis and Brierley*

## Performance Accomplishments

This is the most powerful source of self-confidence that exists in sport. It refers to an athlete's past experiences, and clearly if these have been successful then self-confidence is raised: knowing that you have done something before helps you to believe that you can do it again. This has clear implications for coaching — for example, the progressive development of a skill is important, so in gymnastics if you were working towards a skill on the beam you would ask the gymnast to perform it on the floor first, then on a line on the floor, next on a low beam, and only then on the high beam — but at each stage the athlete's belief in himself is increasing. The message here is, create positive experiences for your athletes: do not set them up in situations for which they are not completely ready because if they fail they will have even less confidence in themselves the next time they try it. Having said that, obviously in sport things do go wrong and mistakes are made — but from every 'bad' performance there is nearly always something that could turn that experience into a positive one. Your job as a coach is to find it!

## Modelling

To enable athletes to perform with greater success, coaches frequently use other athletes as models or to demonstrate an activity. The old saying 'A picture is worth a thousand words' is directly relevant in this case, when the coach or other athletes provide the 'picture'. This can be a very useful source of self-confidence for children, because seeing their friends doing something is quite likely to give them the confidence to have a go too.

## Verbal Persuasion

Often used by coaches to help instil confidence: phrases such as 'You can do it!' or 'Go for it!' suggest to the athletes that they can complete the task. Verbal persuasion can also come from team-mates and parents, and can be beneficial in creating self-efficacy, particularly when learning new skills.

## Emotional Arousal

This refers to a person's ability to control their level of emotional arousal so that it will not adversely affect their performance. It is directly related to cognitive and somatic anxiety, and will be examined later in this chapter when we explore effective coping strategies.

## How the Coach Can Help

It has been demonstrated that clear links exist between cognitive and somatic anxiety, self-confidence and performance. The research indicates that cognitive

*A coach helps an athlete through a difficult time.*

anxiety has an adverse effect on performance, so the more cognitively anxious an athlete becomes the worse his performance will be. Conversely self-confidence has a beneficial effect, so the more confident an athlete feels about his own ability the better his performance will be. The link between somatic anxiety and performance is represented by a curvy linear relationship, suggesting that somatic anxiety can be beneficial but only up to a certain level; beyond this and the symptoms previously described will become a problem for the athlete. It is important that a coach recognizes this process and organizes his training in ways that will help the athlete: by using some of the simple methods suggested below a coach can help to create self-confidence and thereby give his athletes the best possible opportunity for performance success:

- Provide lots of opportunities for the athletes to feel good about themselves
- Reward effort
- Ensure that the athlete has plenty of opportunities to achieve
- Ensure that the last training session before a competition reaffirms the positive aspects of an athlete's abilities
- Set effective goals for competition and training
- Encourage support from within the group of athletes that train together. This is important in both individual and team sports.

## Coping With Anxiety

It is easy for us coaches to recognize when problems are occurring with our athletes which translate into below-par performances. You may now be able to identify that some of these are connected with anxiety or with self-efficacy, and not strictly with the physical or technical aspects of the sport. However, since most coaches concentrate most of the time on improving these aspects of performance, it is not altogether surprising that the athlete will continue to experience difficulties. The good news is that psychological skills can be trained and developed in the same way as technical and physical skills.

In my experience it is important to include the psychological aspect of performance as part of the normal training process — if it is removed from this context then it is viewed as being something altogether separate and its significance can be lost. Indeed, developing these skills during training time is beneficial in more than one way: first, athletes will not question the validity of any of the exercises that you introduce. Second, you will be able to ensure that these skills are worked on — like any skill, in order for it to become effective it must be practised. Third, you will be able to create an atmosphere in training that enables athletes to recognize the mind–body link which will increase awareness about the power of their own mind to control their performance. This holistic approach to performance will stand them in good stead for coping with many situations, sports related or not. So let us examine some different exercises and see how they might be integrated into the training session.

The aim of the exercises is to help athletes develop feelings of being calm and in control, to enable them to restore a sense of balance and a feeling of wellbeing when they feel under pressure. Clearly taking part in any form of competition can cause young athletes to feel stressed, and they will need help in dealing with this. We give here just a few of the exercises that exist; those interested in finding out more about them should look in the 'Self help' section in the local library or bookshop for further reading.

### *Breath Control*

When introducing calming techniques the best way to start is by learning to control the breathing. Breathing is our life force, and the way in which we breathe is often indicative of our state of mind. For example, when we are feeling anxious the pattern of our breathing changes, and it very often becomes shallow or too rapid — in extreme cases of panic we can hyperventilate. The physical effects of shallow breathing include a reduction of oxygen to the brain causing dizziness and headaches; an increase in the amount of calcium released into the tissues, causing heightened sensitivity and 'tingly' sensations; and an increased heart rate, resulting in feelings of tension and apprehension. Our breathing pattern affects our speech, too, and we begin to speak faster and in a more frenetic way. Clearly none of these factors would be conducive to good performance.

For the most part we are not really aware of how we are breathing — if you ask your athletes 'how' they are breathing they might tell you 'in and out' or 'normally' but in fact will probably have little idea exactly what they are doing. However, by learning how to control their breathing they will be able to control the way they feel — so if you do nothing else, teach your athletes breath control, and what is more, practise it yourself: it can be as stressful sitting on the sidelines as it is doing the performing! So how do you develop breath control?

## Developing Breath Control Step by Step

- **Step one:** Find a comfortable place and ask the athlete to lie flat on their back.
- **Step two**: Ask the athlete to place their hands outstretched on their lower abdomen. This will help them to feel exactly how their breathing affects other parts of their body.
- **Step three**: Ask the athlete to distend their abdomen so that it protrudes as far as possible, and then to suck in their stomach as far as possible.
- **Step four**: Get the athlete to notice what happens to their breathing as they do this; in my experience most children will breathe out to distend their stomach and breathe in to suck their stomach in. This is exactly the opposite of what is needed.
- **Step five**: Ask them to follow this breathing pattern: breathe in through the nose as the lower abdomen rises; then breathe out through the mouth as the abdomen falls — the exhalation should be heard. Some people will find this difficult, and they will need to concentrate quite hard in order to achieve it.
- **Step six**: As they breathe in, get them to imagine the air being forced into the extremities of their body.
- **Step seven**: As they breathe out they should feel the tension leave their body.

This exercise can also be carried out standing or sitting; however, in these positions it is important to follow the correct technique; thus:

- The hands should be placed on the hips, with the fingers extended on the abdomen.
- At each inward breath, the shoulders should remain down.
- The chest should not puff out.
- They should feel the abdomen expand as they breathe in.
- The abdomen falls as they breathe out.

You can easily introduce this breathing exercise at the end of a session as part of your cool-down routine. It doesn't have to take very long — the athletes might work for perhaps twenty breaths. Don't worry if at first they find all this too difficult and strange. Often their immediate reaction is to laugh, but persevere, and as they become more familiar with the exercise they will begin to appreciate how helpful it is; then you can leave them to take the initiative as to when they use it. Use verbal cues as you go through the exercise, then whenever they feel tension or anxiety they will know that if they follow this routine they will feel better and calmer — and the calmer your athletes feel, the better they will be able to perform. A word of warning, however: do not expect this to work if the athletes have not spent time working on it: the breath control routine must be as familiar to them as any other part of their training and preparation. Develop it as 'part of the ritual' for your athletes and yourself.

## The Repeating of Affirmations

Another technique that can be used with great effect to help control anxiety is positive self-statement, otherwise known as the repeating of affirmations. It calls upon the subconscious mind, a powerful force which can be used to help or hinder us. The essential difference between the subconscious and the conscious mind is that the subconscious mind cannot distinguish between fact and fiction; all it can do is act upon the force of the suggestion. For example, tell yourself often enough that you feel sick and sure enough your body will start to respond; in a sports setting one of the most common must be when children tell themselves that they 'can't do something'. They repeat it so often that they convince their subconscious that this is the reality — so when they do try to do whatever it is, not surprisingly they can't. Moreover, unless their thinking changes, their ability to do it will remain impaired. Much of cognitive anxiety is a result of the subconscious working overtime on the wrong things. But the good news is that the subconscious can just as easily be harnessed to work powerfully as a positive force — all it needs is a bit of encouragement!

So how can we apply this principle to sport? The key to success when using applied suggestion is to ensure that the suggestion is acceptable to the subconscious: as long as it is, the subconscious will set about transforming it into reality.

## Creating and Using Affirmations Step by Step

• **Step one**: First use the breath control routine to create an internal state of calm.
• **Step two**: Ask the athlete to develop a phrase or saying that encapsulates what they want to be like. Make sure that the words used in the phrase have the following characteristics:
   1. They reflect how the athlete would ideally like to be.
   2. They are positive and to the point.
   3. They are in the present tense
   4. They are active rather than passive.
   5. They appeal to the imagination.
• **Step three**: The athlete must repeat these words over and over again; this

can be made even more effective if they are said out loud and into a mirror. The important thing in this exercise is the repetition, because the more the phrase is repeated, the more powerful it will become.The following are some examples of powerful affirmations:

> *I have the power, the strength and the knowledge to handle everything.*
> *I am calm and in control.*
> *I feel total confidence in my skills and abilities.*
> *I feel strong and full of vitality.*
> *I can achieve anything that I want to.*

If an athlete has difficulty deciding on their own affirmation, ask them to identify the cause of their anxiety, then to think up an affirmation that is the exact opposite of it. For instance if they are feeling depressed, then the affirmation needs to state that they feel uplifted; if they are feeling tense, then the affirmation should state that they feel really calm; if they doubt their own ability to achieve their goal, then the affirmation must state that they can do it easily. As with the breath control exercise, the longer the athlete works with the technique, the more effective it will become.

Affirmations can be used and applied in a hundred different ways: during the week leading up to an important competition, as a part of the preparation ritual; to help develop confidence before a new skill is tried; and during competition as well as during training.

## Postural Relaxation

A common symptom of anxiety is increased muscle tension — although very often it is not recognized as such until someone else points it out. For some people this tension is apparent around the shoulders and neck, for others it exists in clenched jaws or their hands. Exercises which address this might be referred to as postural relaxation exercises, and essentially what they do is change the posture in order to reduce the tension. The following are simple but very effective, the key being for the athlete to recognize the symptoms so that the most effective technique can be applied:

1. For jaw clenchers: To reduce the tension in the jaw simply part the lips slightly and rest the tongue gently on the roof of the mouth just behind the front teeth. Feel the tension in the jaw relax. To maximize effectiveness use with the breath control exercise.

2. For fist clenchers: Shake out the hands to release the tension. Then gently place the fingers of one hand on top of the other with the palms facing upwards. Make the thumb tips of each hand gently touch. Assume this position whilst using the breath control exercise.

3. Walk tall:   Change the whole posture of the body so that it describes one of total confidence: chin lifted, straight back, shoulders down and relaxed. It is amazing how simply changing your posture will affect the way you feel.

4. Facial expression:  Remove facial tension by lifting the eyebrows and opening the eyes. A lot of anxiety is held in a frown, so remove it and you will immediately feel better.

These are very simple techniques, which can be practised and used at any time, anywhere. It is the coach's task to make them a part of normal training and competition preparation, because then athletes will be committed to them and will reap the rewards.

## In Conclusion

This chapter has focused on some of the key psychological factors that can directly influence the performance of young athletes. Unfortunately most coaching awards focus on teaching coaches the technical skills and physical requirements of their sport — rarely are they taught about the psychological factors that relate to performance, or what they can do about them. Indisputably coaching is complex, it is really an art that applies science, and in order to be effective coaches need to understand and apply a whole range of scientific parameters. It is crucial that both the sport science community and the coaching community should recognize this.

# CHAPTER NINE

# Winning Isn't Everything

Sports performers need to understand how to do well in competitions, or at least how to evaluate a negative outcome so that they can plan for future success. This is not always as easy as it sounds, possibly because of the mystique which seems to surround the subject. There appears to be little analysis of how to use time effectively in the build-up to a match or competition in order to maximize performance. But this need not be the case. By considering what is different about the competition process we may develop a better guide as to how training should be modified to allow performers to compete better.

## The Physical Demands of Competition

There is no doubt that the competition process appears daunting for some and draining for others; possibly these perceptions are based on real situations, but equally they may have arisen because of a lack of success, rather than because of constructive consideration of what is involved. So let us consider the organization of competitions in order to understand in what ways they are similar.

### Transport and Travel Arrangements

Whether the match is at home or away will have obvious implications for those responsible for transport and travel arrangements. First of all you need to know whether the starting time is fixed or subject to change in order to work out how long to allow beforehand to accomplish all the preliminary tasks such as checking in, finding out specific organization details, checking kit, liaising with coaches, managers and physiotherapists, checking the environmental conditions, and relaxing. This is certainly true when playing at home, and those travelling to a new venue should allow themselves extra time to locate all the facilities, such as the changing room, the officials' room, medical area, toilets, ticket office if required, warm-up area and reporting procedures. This will probably mean that a visiting team or individual will want to arrive 90 minutes before the start time, depending on how long they estimate it will take to report in and to warm up.

When estimating the total travel time you should also allow for finding the venue, local parking difficulties, the town-to-town distance, the number of home town pick-ups, and a bit extra for late arrivals. Because of the vagaries of evening and weekend travel, for journeys over twenty-five miles it is probably best to allow an hour more than you estimate is needed.

Once you have worked out how long it will probably take to get to the match venue, and how much preparation time will be needed, it can then be decided how best to organize travel plans in relation to assisting performance.

There is no doubt that performers must be physically ready to compete, and ideally they will have done a certain amount to prepare themselves — they will have slept well, they will be rested from training and work, and they will have high levels of energy reserve. However, this is not always as simple as it might seem. For instance, the amount of sleep an individual needs to function at his best varies enormously — so whilst we know that, in general, children need more sleep than those in middle age, this doesn't necessarily apply to all within those two age groups. Moreover the extra demands placed upon those involved in intensive training in sport, with the associated need to recover quickly, will further complicate matters. However, some general conclusions regarding travel arrangements can be reached.

First you will have to decide whether it would be all right to travel on the day, or if it would be better to travel the day before; this will depend on how far away the competition is, and how well a performer competes after travelling. Most premier football clubs consider that if the journey will take more than three hours, it is best to stay overnight en route, even if the kick-off is in the afternoon. On the other hand, clubs in the lower echelons will not have the finances to allow this on more than the longest of journeys. However, for a particularly important competition it may make all the difference to the players to budget in advance in order to make this possible.

Those performers who can relax, rest and even sleep well whilst travelling are lucky, and will be able catch up on any bed rest they may have missed in the foregoing week. Take pillows, travel cushions and blankets to help them in this, as well as a good supply of relaxing music and reading material. Avoid loud music and computer games: these stimulate the nervous system and are better left for those occasions when lethargic performers need a bit of a motivational boost in the course of a long season.

## Staying Overnight

It is also important to take into account whether a performer is a morning person or a night owl: an all-day tournament could well get off to a bad start if their body clock has not been conditioned to an early morning match or qualifying round. Most people are aware of when they are most productive, and they may need to adapt their training times in order to be at their best for a competition with an unusual start time. The general rule of thumb that what you do on a competition day should be no different from what you would normally do on a training day is especially applicable here. Therefore it would be a good idea to schedule at least two training sessions at the specific start time, even if they are more of a conditioning or fitness session. Even if there is no facility for skill training, this should not preclude some form of practice at match time.

Going to bed early the evening before a match in order to get a good night's sleep may leave you tossing and turning if you are not used to it. It may therefore be best to advise players to go to sleep at the usual time, but having done rather less work and taken rather more rest during the day. Sleeping at home is preferable as it maintains the normal routine, but if players do stay overnight, certain practical considerations should be borne in mind — having gone to the trouble of booking a hotel room somewhere, do not ruin their chances of a good night's sleep by complications which could be anticipated. For example, choose a quiet room away from busy roads with heavy curtains to block out street lights. Check that the beds will be long enough for your taller competitors, and that pillows are of the right type for those who suffer respiratory problems. Take a supply of eye masks and ear plugs in case there are room mates who need a light on, or who snore. Finally, arrange for a wake-up call to be doubly certain of being up in time; and find out the breakfast menu so that alternative arrangements can be made for those requiring special diets.

## What to Eat and Drink

On match day, breakfast is the most important meal — as it is on any other training day for that matter. Cereals, toast, good quality jams, fruit juice and water should be central to what is consumed; tea, coffee and fried food should be avoided: they may feature in some star performers' autobiographies but they are probably best kept to a minimum since caffeine acts as a diuretic thus dehydrating the body, and cooked meals have a high fat and protein content which can upset the digestion, cause further dehydration, and reduce the amounts of carbohydrate which can be consumed. Generally performers should be encouraged to eat as much as they normally would — although it is to be expected that pre-competition nerves will cause a loss of appetite for some.

A supply of bottled water, bananas and carbohydrate snacks are useful to 'top up with' during the period after the last meal and in the one to two hours before competition commences. If a performer has trained with isotonic sports drinks without previous reaction then he might continue to take them with impunity; otherwise the rule about 'nothing new' would apply here. Drinking regularly — and this would equate to a cup of water every 15 minutes in the two hours before competition — is the best way to ensure that you do not feel thirsty. Whilst this is obvious advice, thirst does not just indicate a desire to drink, but suggests that dehydration is already a factor. Keeping hydration levels high is important as it directly affects the function of the nervous system, and this in turn controls our decision-making capabilities, our co-ordination and mental control — indeed, it has recently been estimated that as little as a 1 per cent hydration loss through sweating can reduce performance by up to 10 per cent. As opportunities to drink during competition are more limited, the only solution is what might appear to be 'over drinking' in the build-up.

## How to 'Kill Time'

Knowing how to keep yourself occupied in the time leading up to the start of your team's warm-up is a skill which improves the more you are in that particular situation. It is a good idea to have a plan of what you will and will not do, and in roughly what order you will do things.

Inexperienced performers often walk around or stand up too much, thus needlessly tiring themselves before they have started. Others get bored and then eat too much, or start their individual warm-up too early. The opposite scenario is also true, when people leave late because they have underestimated journey time or have slept too late, and then have to conduct a hurried warm-up. Ideally what you do should involve a minimum of activity with maximum rest, hydration and physical relaxation. A short walk and a stretch immediately after a journey is nevertheless useful, as long as it is short. Reading books, talking about non-competition matters or listening to music keeps players' attention off the task at hand until such time as we have planned to start our focus on what we have to do.

Packing all the necessary kit and equipment is better done the day before a competition. A large, easily recognized waterproof bag with several compartments is essential, as is a written checklist of things to pack. Different things will need to be taken to cover all the eventualities involved in travel, preparation, the competition itself and the post-competition period, and forgetting one important thing could seriously compromise your concentration as you prepare. Money, contact details, food, wet weather gear, change of clothes, simple medical supplies, music systems and the like are important, as well as all the competition-related kit.

## How Much to Train

In the forty-eight hours immediately before the competition it is important that heavy intensive training is drastically reduced. The body stores carbohydrate, its preferred fuel source for sports requiring speed and power, as glycogen in the liver and working muscles. The stores at muscle level are released for immediate all-out effort but are quickly used up, upon which the liver supplies are released directly into the bloodstream as a second wave. Therefore it is important that the levels of both are as high as possible immediately before a competition, particularly if players are involved in a tournament, or if qualifier and final take place on the same day. This process of building up the body's reserves — rather like recharging a battery— takes the equivalent of two days, and is best accomplished without the drain that hard training would inevitably cause.

Medium duration training, with selected elements at high intensity, will allow players to train at match speed but for shorter periods of time. Stretching and recovery work with bursts of high speed activities are better compromises later in the week; and massage, mental training, developing tactical under-standing and light technical work can also be undertaken at this time.

This is no more than a cursory look at the very complex issue of competition preparation; nevertheless it does highlight the fact that people who should do well at competitions sometimes do not. If we then attempt to analyse exactly what happened, and to assess how helpful the preparation was, we may better understand how to prepare for future events. Compared to training days, com-petition days are far more different than people anticipate; therefore we must think more carefully about the competitions themselves so that we use the information to plan our training, rather than training in the hope that the com-petitions will go well.

## The Psychological Demands of Competition

Why is it that an athlete can train brilliantly, demonstrate excellent technical and physical skills, and yet when it comes to a competition all of these abilities seem to desert him? Clearly it is the competition situation itself that makes this occur: the technical and physical abilities of an athlete cannot simply vanish in the space of twenty-four hours — however, the self-belief and confidence can, and this is often the reason for under-performance. There are certain key situa-tional differences between competition and training, and these need to be explored in order to determine effective strategies for dealing with them: although some of them might seem obvious, they are still worth mentioning. One is the fact that competition is a public assessment of the athlete's abilities: he will be labelled as a success or failure — there is nowhere to hide.

In the past it was thought that athletes were either good competitors, or they were not, and there was nothing that could be done about it — but in fact this is really not the case. Psychological skills can be taught in preparation for com-petition in the same way as any other skill in sport. In this section we will explore the psychological pitfalls that an athlete may encounter.

### The Week Before

An athlete can begin to feel cognitive competitive anxiety long before the com-petition, and this is particularly true of those who do not compete on a weekly basis. These feelings can be associated with fear of the unknown, lack of self-confidence, and self-doubt, to name but a few, and if an athlete is experiencing this sort of thing it will have a direct influence on how he performs. It is there-fore important for him to remember that 'you are what you think' — so he is much more likely to perform well when he feels he is in control of the situation. The job of the coach is to maximize the situations in which an athlete can feel this, so let us look more practically at the options available.

## Performance Accomplishments

We have seen from the section in Chapter 8 that performance accomplishments are critical to the feeling of self-efficacy of any performer, and it is crucial to exploit this during the week before the competition. In practical terms this means that as a competition approaches, the training sessions should highlight the strengths of the athletes: allow them to feel as if 'they can', by reinforcing the excellent skills that you know they possess. Do not introduce new skills or tactics just before a competition, because this could risk damaging their confidence in their own ability. In 'closed' sports such as gymnastics, skating and diving this must be observed even more closely.

## Competition Desensitization

As previously mentioned, the greater control that an athlete feels he has, the better his performance will be. This can be achieved by creating an atmosphere which is as much like the one prevailing at the competition as possible. An example of this is the England rugby team, who identified that one of the difficult factors associated with playing Wales at home would be the overwhelming singing, which was bound to distract the team performance. However, by training with a sound-track of the singing they became desensitized to it, and were then back in control of the situation. Indeed, there are many situations that occur in competition to which an athlete needs to become desensitized; consider the following: refereeing decisions that go against them, making a false start, making a mistake, being judged — these are just a few. The point that needs to come across is that if an athlete has practised under those conditions, when they occur in competition he will have experienced it already, and will therefore feel that he is still in control. Examine a situation for yourself and devise an appropriate training for your athletes.

## What If ...

Give your athletes the opportunity to discuss the competitions fully, with all the possible nightmare scenarios. Now you might think that this is strange — why on earth would you want to discuss the negative? Well, this does a number of things: first, it means the athletes can share their fears with you and the team, and this is very healthy, engendering greater understanding and support amongst your performers. Secondly, it allows you to discuss some 'coping' strategies. Many of the fears that athletes have are unfounded, but they are nevertheless real to them, and as such can be detrimental to performance. By finding realistic solutions the athletes will feel as if they are in control of the situation, and this is very important as it helps them maintain high levels of self-confidence. Talk to your athletes about what they like and dislike; be sure you are clear about what they want, and what they expect from you and their other team-mates. For example, some athletes want you to be with them, others need time by themselves to prepare. If you have not asked them what they want and need, how can you get it right?

## Goal-Setting

Be sure that all the athletes have set themselves clear goals (see Chapter 5). It is important that these goals relate to the performance, and not just to the outcome. Make this a formal process; it will become critical for the competition evaluation.

## Checklists

Provide a checklist for parents that has all the relevant information on it. Include details such as the kit that will be worn, and the venue of the competition with maps, timing of events and food requirements. The more information parents have, the better prepared they can be.

## The Night Before

The night before any competition can often be very difficult for young athletes. Firstly, they believe that they need extra sleep to ensure that they are ready for the competition (this is probably what they have been told to do by their coach). This would appear to make perfect sense, but remember that in order for the athlete to feel in control, he needs to follow a familiar routine. So if this normally means going to bed at 10pm, and he goes to bed at 9pm for extra sleep, the chances are fairly high that because his normal routine is altered, he will stay awake — and awake he is more likely to be focusing on the competition and possibly negative aspects associated with it. So the extra sleep the athletes thought they were getting often doesn't materialize, and the self doubts that can creep in can wreak havoc on performance.. The mind is a very powerful tool: you can talk yourself into and out of anything, so it is important that the last thoughts an athlete has are positive ones.

If an athlete has problems getting to sleep before a competition, the following useful tips may be tried:

• Relaxation exercises( it doesn't really matter which one, as long as the athlete is familiar with it).

• The use of essential oils can help you get to sleep. Try putting a few drops of an oil such as lavender in a bath before going to sleep — it can help immensely. (For more information on the use of aromatherapy there are many excellent books now available on the market.)

• Use positive affirmations (see Chapter 8).

•   Use positive imagery related to the competition. Encourage the athlete to visualize in as much detail as possible themselves competing with a positive outcome; if they can do it in their own mind they are well on their way.

•   Do final equipment checks. Encourage your athletes to pack their bag the night before; this will give them plenty of time to ensure that they have everything that they need, and that it is all in good working order: it is better to discover the night before if something needs attention rather than on the day of the competition. Encourage athletes to be responsible for their own kit. This forms part of a familiar routine, again helping the athlete to feel in control.

## *The Day of the Competition*

It is most important for an athlete that competition day should not bring any unexpected surprises. Try to get your athletes to develop their own competition routine, one that they become familiar and comfortable with. It is often the little things that become really important to an athlete, and if these are not right, their whole day can be tipped off balance. So if it is wearing those lucky socks, then go with it!

Here are a few more ideas that can help athletes compete at their best. Encourage them to:

•   Start the day with the right attitude — smiling helps. Use positive affirmations (see Chapter 8) to set the right tone for what follows.

•   Allow enough time for arrival and acclimatization to the competition arena. Be pro-active as a coach, talk and walk through the environment, and identify what the athletes need to become aware of. Don't assume that they have figured everything out for themselves. Last-minute panics because they can't find the loo cause unnecessary anxiety.

•   Use a familiar warm-up routine. All the athletes should know exactly what they need to do to prepare physically, and how long they need to do this.

•   Use mental rehearsal at an appropriate time prior to competing, to enhance self-confidence.

•   Use the breath control technique (see Chapter 8) whenever athletes start to feel jittery and nervous. Controlling the breathing should be the last thing they do before they compete.

•   Tell athletes to 'feel the fear, and do it anyway....'

## The Psychology of Injury

The incidence of an injury at some point in an athlete's sporting life is almost inevitable, and at that moment much of what he has been working towards is struck away at a stroke. Whether an injury is minor or serious, the challenge that is presented to the athlete not only revolves around recovering physically, but also psychologically and emotionally. Moreover, the way in which he is treated throughout this process will have a direct influence on the extent and speed of his recovery.

Whilst injury is about the body being damaged, there is also now a growing body of research that makes it clear that there may also be emotional and psychological damage, which is often overlooked. By enhancing their understanding of the recovery process, coaches can ensure that they provide better support and empathy for their athletes.

The main finding from current research is that the process an injured athlete experiences is similar to that of the grief process. You might think that this seems a little extreme: after all, it is only an injury, not a life or death situation. But consider this from a semi-pro footballer, responding just after he had been injured.

'As soon as I went down I knew it was serious.....Back in the changing room on my own I felt despair. I could not go through this again. I felt so hollow and isolated. My silent grieving was just beginning...'  Or this from another injured athlete: 'I feel so empty...it's like I have lost something, and just don't know when it will return. It is a fear I cannot explain — it just will not leave me.'

The grief response is apparent in any situation where there is an identifiable loss. In the case of the injured athlete it is the loss of being unable to participate in activity which they clearly love; it can also be the loss of the athlete's identity if his sport defines who he is — in such cases the injury can really create emotional havoc. Established psychological research into the grieving process recognizes that an individual passes through identifiable stages, and the athlete also passes through these stages on the way to recovery. Let us explore these in more detail:

* *Denial* : This is the first stage experienced by the athlete, and it is often characterized by such statements as 'There's no problem', or 'I'm fine, really I am'. But when the realization hits them that there really is something wrong, and the implications that this has for them in terms of their competitive future, denial is quickly replaced by anger.

* *Anger* : The second stage is characterized by statements such as 'Why me?' and the desire to somehow retaliate for what has happened. The targets for these angry outbursts are often immediate family or the coach and team-mates. The anger is due to the fact that they can no longer perform or participate.

* *Bargaining*: During this stage the athlete often tries to avoid the reality of the

situation by setting up unrealistic promises; for example: 'If I recover quickly from this I will always train really hard'; or 'If I recover from this I will be really nice to my coach.'

• *Depression*: This stage is often the hardest for the athlete to come to terms with, since it is caused by the realization that nothing can be done, and that there is uncertainty about the future. It is often accompanied by extreme mood swings, as this quote indicates: 'One minute I'm in a good mood, the next I get really depressed and irritable!' — or this from an athlete who has been told that it will take a minimum of six weeks before he can play again: 'My moods are going from bad to worse — I'm still finding it hard, and feel as if I'm making no progress. During the night my moods have hit an all-time low. I'm so depressed...' If an athlete gets stuck at this stage it can severely hinder the healing process. An athlete who is constantly re-affirming the negative with negative self-statements or negative images will only prolong the depression, and in turn the injury. The healing process begins in the mind, the body simply follows.

• *Acceptance*: Once an athlete reaches this stage he will be ready for rehabilitation and return to the sport; if he can begin to recognize progress, however small, then he is well on his way.

Whilst it is clear that most athletes will pass through all these stages, there are huge variations in the length of time that he will remain at any one particular stage. This will depend on a number of factors, namely the athlete himself, the severity of the injury and also its consequence (ie will it keep him out for a few weeks, or months, or will he never be able to return) and the support systems that are in place. So let us examine some practical ways in which an athlete can be helped through this difficult time:

• Recognize that the athlete will be experiencing a difficult time both physically and emotionally. Be prepared to absorb some of his anger when it is thrown in your direction, rather than reacting to it and thereby intensifying the situation.

• Do not isolate the athlete. This is often a common problem for those who are injured: suddenly they are no longer included, they are no longer part of the team. They feel as if they are redundant, and this is often reinforced by coaches who say 'Come back when you're fit'; often the only support that the athlete may be receiving is from a physiotherapist. If a coach is to help provide good social support to the injured athlete, he must keep in regular contact and should look for situations where the injured party can still contribute something — maybe he could help out in some way, perhaps through coaching younger athletes, or at least by doing something else that makes them feel valued and still part of the squad.

• Do use goal-setting strategies; these will help the athlete to recover. Apply the same principles as designated in Chapter 5, but make them specific to rehabilitation; in this way the athlete will be better able to recognize progress. This is enormously beneficial to their self-confidence, as well as to their injury. Goal-setting is also helpful in ensuring that athletes don't do too much too soon and re-injure themselves in the process.

• Do use visualization. There is a lot of evidence that by using positive visualization of healing taking place an individual will experience a faster recovery. Much of this evidence has come from the treatment of cancer patients, where individuals have been taught visualization skills as part of their treatment.

• Do get the athlete to use the relaxation techniques outlined in Chapter 8. If he is stressed as well as injured, then this will impact on the recovery process. Often the hardest time can be at night, especially in the early stages of an injury when the pain seems to intensify. By employing an appropriate relaxation technique an athlete will be able to manage his injury more effectively.

• Do encourage the athlete to think positively. Utilize effective thought-stopping techniques, so that every time an athlete says something negative you make him re-phrase it using a positive statement. For example an athlete says, 'I feel awful, I am never going to get any better': this can be re-phrased to emphasize the positive progress that has already been made.

## Physical Aspects of Injury

Competition is important in that it tests the degree of training effectiveness. Yet as a yardstick to judge competence, its requirements are seldom given sufficient consideration. By analysing the general preparation for competition, as well as the specific performance and outcome, children can start to believe in their abilities as worthy contenders. Coaches need to encourage children to evaluate more consistently the causes of competition success and failure, and to liaise with parents so that they may provide effective support and advice in the pre-contest period.

# CHAPTER TEN

# A Whole New Ball Game ...

A triangular relationship appears to exist in sport between the coach, the athlete and the parent. Whilst this may suggest that there is an equal relationship between all three, it also infers that there should be equal dialogue between all parties. When children are involved, and especially when they are competing in sport, it is important that this relationship works. We have already discussed many areas that can be utilized to enhance the relationship between the coach and the athlete, so let us consider the nature of that between the coach and the parent.

## The Coach–Parent Relationship

Ask many coaches to identify their main irritation and they will often tell you that 'The kids are fine, it's just their parents that are the problem'. The parents, however, can be made to feel sidelined by the coach, as if they have no more value than as a chauffeur. Clearly the relationship between the coach and the parent is a potential source of conflict, but if the child is to gain the most from sport – and especially competitive sport – then there must be respect and understanding from both parties. So let us examine some of the main sources of conflict, and some resolutions.

## The Side-Line Coach

The parent who becomes the side-line coach during training sessions – or worse still, during a competition – can create real problems for the coach. This involves the parent offering their child 'advice' and voicing their opinion which may or may not be in agreement with what the coach is saying. This will undermine the coach and probably totally confuse the child who will not know who to listen to, and it is clearly essential to define roles and expectations – if nothing else, the parent needs to trust the coach and to recognize that they have the appropriate knowledge and expertise. So how can this be best achieved ?

A 'code of conduct' contract can be drawn up, which details what the coach will do, what the athlete is expected to do, and what the parent is expected to do. This can then be signed and agreed to by all parties so it makes it clear how everyone is expected to behave. This can be especially useful for coaches of team sports where real problems appear to exist with parents abusing referees or the opposing team. The code of conduct could itemize in writing that such behaviour is unacceptable, and that it will result in the withdrawal of the parent, and possibly the child, from the competition. If this is made clear from the start then it is much easier to deal with problems when they arise because there is a framework already in place that everyone has agreed to.

If drawing up such a contract is considered to be too extreme a measure to take, a meeting might be held at the beginning of a term with all the athletes and the parents, and the issues raised in the same way. What is important is that there is universal acceptance of the code of conduct.

## *The Exclusion of Parents*

Parents who feel as if they are totally excluded will often feel disgruntled, and rightly so. Coaches need to be aware that parents provide the lifeline to the athlete and without their willingness to get them to training sessions, take them to competitions and generally re-organize their lives so that the athlete can participate, the coach would have no children to coach. Furthermore, a parent has the right to be involved, and to be fully informed as to the progress that their child is making. You would not expect a child to go through school without having regular reports, or the opportunity to meet and discuss things with the teacher, so why should it be any different for sport? Parents want to know how their child is getting on, even if he or she is simply participating in recreational level sport on a weekly basis, and it is the coach's responsibility to ensure that the parents are given enough feedback. This can be provided in a number of ways, some informal – for instance, chatting to parents after a session – or formal, by way of a written report, or by setting aside a designated time to discuss relevant issues with the parent. This is even more effective if the parent knows exactly what the coach is planning for that athlete – the goal-setting planners in Chapter 5 can help with this – because they can then see if they are reaching the goals and generally improving. It is really important that coaches establish effective lines of communication between athletes and parents. If parents feel they can trust the coach, then they are more likely to be supportive.

## *Expectations*

Both parents and coach can be unrealistic in their expectations, and again, this can be a source of conflict. Parents very often find it hard to agree upon the time spent training, the arrangements for training and competition, and the financial commitment.

First of all, parents will have a natural concern that their child is spending too much time training and not enough time on school work. This is perfectly understandable, given that only a tiny percentage of athletes will be able to make a living from actually performing their sport, so the coach needs to be able to reassure the parent that a sensible balance between the two will be made. The coach needs to be aware of important times in the academic calendar, and to allow the athlete enough time to concentrate on school rather than sport. If the athlete is very talented and is involved in elite level competition it may be appropriate to discuss the situation with the school and to explain what the demands are likely to be from the sport. I have done this, and have found that if the school is fully appraised of the situation it is more likely to be supportive to the athlete.

The second issue relates to arrangements for training and competition, and in this it is vital that coaches keep parents informed. They must remember that parents have to juggle many things, and if training is suddenly changed or a competition suddenly announced, they should not be too surprised when parents either don't meet the new arrangements, or moan about them being changed. Give advanced warning!

Thirdly, parents are often reluctant to make a big financial commitment, whether it be buying that new kit or buying new trainers if the child has just begun in the sport. Only if there is real commitment should these extra financial burdens be placed on the child.

Coaches and parents can best support each other by mutual understanding of roles and responsibilities. The following list provides a starting point for this process:

### What Coaches Need from Parents
- To believe in their children, and help the children believe in themselves.
- To avoid putting unnecessary pressure on their children.
- To help their children to accept success with humility.
- To help their children to cope with defeat with grace and renewed determination to succeed.
- To support the efforts of the coach regardless of team performance.
- To be supportive and understanding when competitions are not going well.
- To provide help for the coach (videoing, observation, scoring).
- To provide information on sleep, mood, nutrition and schoolwork for wider evaluation.
- To help the coach keep a sense of perspective.

### What Parents Need from Coaches
- To treat their children with care, compassion and respect.
- To make their children better people as well as better players.
- To value their children's input and opinion.
- To train their children in a manner that is conversant with their age, experience, ability and aspiration.
- To understand, value and positively represent them with their children.
- To explain how they can best support the coach.
- To be treated and educated in a professional manner in their respective supporting role.
- To be advised when there is a problem, to be given a chance to discuss it,

and to share in the solution.
* To actively believe that a team-based approach can, and will work.

Assuming that this very important supportive group can help the young performer, their combined expertise may now appear to be lacking. This is not an intended criticism, but a product of expected improvement because as competitors learn more about how to improve they often develop more insight than their parents, and eventually even their coach. It is at this point that the coach may start to assume the role of training adviser and talent manager and that performers and coaches increasingly need to consider recruiting specialists with particular expertise. This will provide information to help with the planning of future training, and will also boost motivation and interest. At this stage it is worth considering what some of these specializations offer, as well as looking at other relevant support providers.

## Sport Science Support

Until quite recently the science of sport has only existed as a vehicle for research in universities, and useful information was therefore not easily accessible to those coaches and athletes who needed it. However, this scenario has now begun to change, mainly as a result of the vision of the National Coaching Foundation (NCF) who realized that if there was to be an improvement in the standards of athletic performance then they had to improve the access to sport science for coaches: this, they maintained, was the only way to improve the general level of their knowledge and understanding. The series of courses that were developed by the NCF were directly related to the range of professional needs identified by active coaches. This provided a useful development for National Governing Bodies (NGBs) of sport who did have their own coach education programmes, even if these were rarely related to specific sports science knowledge. The 'sport sciences' is a term used to describe a number of different sub-disciplines, all of which are concerned with the study of sport through scientific means. Throughout this book we have been applying scientific theory to support the information presented, and it is important that coaches are aware of the different disciplines and what they have to offer.

## Sports Biomechanics

This discipline focuses on the detailed examination of movement patterns. By using very sophisticated video analysis techniques, scientists can explore the most effective way to perform a given skill. This can be very helpful to coaches if they want to have the skills of their athlete analysed to see if these can be improved and made more efficient. Biomechanics has had a considerable part to play in the development of sports that have a high technical component, such as gymnastics or throwing events.

## Sports Physiology

Sports physiology or exercise physiology is concerned with developing a better understanding of body function. For example, scientists from this discipline investigate such areas as how the body functions under different training regimes, or how it copes with different climates. This type of information has proved invaluable for coaches who have had to prepare athletes for competition in extreme heat such as the 1996 Atlanta Olympics.

## Sports Psychology

Sports psychologists are concerned with trying to understand the psychological factors that will affect an athlete's performance. This has perhaps been one of the areas that the sports community finds hardest to accept as being valuable to coaches, probably due to the association with mental disorder and the stigma attached to this. But the work of sports psychologists researches many areas, including the better understanding of motivation, group cohesion and anxiety, to name a few. This discipline can help coaches in a variety of ways, including the developing of psychological skills necessary for excellent performance.

## Sports Nutrition

Sports nutritionists have an important role in advising athletes on correct eating habits to maximize performance. These experts identify the specific energy needs of any one sport, and help to draw up appropriate diets for the athletes concerned. For example the calorific needs of a marathon runner are completely different from those of a diver, and obviously the diet needs to reflect this. Sports nutrition information can also be very helpful in those sports where athletes have to make a certain weight category, and need to be advised about how this can be safely achieved.

   All these disciplines now contribute directly to the development of sport in this country. The need for coaches to have easy access to these scientists is being achieved through the different sports councils, the NCF and the British Olympic Association who are constantly trying to bridge the gaps between the academics and practitioners, and to enhance our 'appliance of science'.

## The Youth Sport Trust

The Youth Sport Trust (YST) is a relatively new organization created in 1994 to work in partnership with the sports councils and the NCF. Unlike other sports organizations, its sole aim is to develop and implement quality sports programmes for children between four and eighteen years. The Youth Sport Trust cites its aims as being to provide the following for all children:
- fun and success in sport;
- top coaching and top resources;

- an introduction to sport suited to their own level of development;
- the opportunity to develop a range of sports skills;
- the chance to develop good sporting attitudes;
- positive competition;
- a sound foundation for lifelong physical activity.

Because the YST is so young its impact has not been fully felt yet, but this will surely change because the key to future success undoubtedly lies in the approach that it is taking. It recognizes that in order to be effective its programmes must be delivered in both schools and communities, and the range of programmes it has developed reflects this.

## YST Programme

**TOP Play**: This caters for four- to nine-year-olds; the focus is on core sports skills such as throwing, kicking, running and jumping. The main emphasis on the delivery is that the children must have fun, and the aim is to deliver these programmes in primary schools and play centres. The YST provides training and resources for teachers, and equipment to enable a quality delivery.

**TOP Sport**: This focuses on introducing games and sport to seven- to eleven-year-olds. Key sports have been identified for the delivery of this programme, and again training and resources are provided to ensure quality.

**Champion Coaching**: This is aimed at improving performance by providing trained coaches and youth sport managers to work in the community delivering quality sports programmes. This has already proved to be very successful, with currently over 100,000 children and 10,000 coaches involved.

**TOP Club**: This is designed to assist existing clubs deliver better programmes in a wide diversity of sports. This programme is seen as being crucial to the long-term sporting success of the UK because it is considered that providing such valuable assistance to clubs will help enormously in the development of junior potential.

## The Lottery Sports Fund

Sport is one of the five 'good causes' that benefits from money raised by the National Lottery. The Lottery Sports Fund is distributed by the English Sports Council, the Scottish Sports Council and the sports councils for Wales and Northern Ireland, and is divided according to the population of each of the home countries.

Originally the Sports Fund could only be used for building and improving sports facilities, but in 1996 changes were introduced to help talented individuals and teams to improve their international ranking and performance. The

World Class Performance Programme aims to produce significant improvements in Olympic, Commonwealth and European championships. It provides indirect support through awards to the national governing bodies to develop sports coaching and talent identification projects at both grass-roots and elite levels, whilst also providing direct support for talented individuals.

National governing bodies of sport can apply for the funding that will assist with the implementation of their performance plans – that is, the training and preparation of members of junior and senior national squads for international competition. This could include up to 90 per cent of the cost of activities such as the employment of coaches and team/squad managers for elite performers, sports medicine and sports science support programmes, training facilities and equipment, warm weather and acclimatization programmes as well as attendance at major competitions.

The subsistence awards for individual sportsmen and women are designed to provide personal financial support for athletes so they can maintain appropriate training standards and competition programmes in accordance with their needs. This assessment takes into account personal expenditure on items such as food and special diets, living accommodation and regular travel for training or competition purposes. The level of help will depend on the individual's personal circumstances, and his or her current level of achievement and competitive standing. In order to qualify for a subsistence award individuals must be identified by their national governing body and fit into either the 'elite category' ie the top ten world-ranked individuals, or the top four teams; or the 'international category', ie the top twenty individuals and the top eight teams; or the 'national category', ie they must be a member of an international squad.

## National Vocational Qualifications

Coach development includes the recruitment, employment and deployment of coaches, but at the centre is coach education. Coaches themselves have become increasingly aware that there is more to coaching than the technical aspects of their own sport, and developments in coach education over the last decade have stemmed from the belief that they need to be able to access the ever-increasing performance-related knowledge that is available through sports science. In addition, many coaches believe that they can benefit from the greater professionalization of their coaching activities; indeed, career pathways for coaches have been slowly emerging in a range of sports.

An important element in the evolution of coach education in recent years has been the development of sport-based 'National Vocational Qualifications', known as NVQs (or SNVQs in Scotland). S/NVQs are based on occupational standards set by the industry lead body, in this case the National Training Organization for Sport, Recreation and Allied Occupations (SPRITO). NVQs provide a benchmark for a number of areas of the sports industry, including coaching. Although they may be considered relatively expensive (approximately £100 an NVQ), people working in either a voluntary or a paid capacity can gain a qualification that is becoming more widely recognized by employers in the UK and in Europe. In some cases, certain employers may insist on a coaching qualification being NVQ-approved.

S/NVQs may be taken on their own, or alongside any other traditional qualification; in practice they tend to be taken in addition to National Governing Body (NGB) awards. NVQs differ from other qualifications in that they are about how well a coach carries out his/her job against the standards set by the S/NVQ. There are no grades or pass marks, rather there is an assessment of units of competence, that is the tasks that demonstrate a practical ability to do an effective job. Competence is a combination of five factors: skill, knowledge, attitude, self-confidence and perception. In order to gain an NVQ, the coach will been seen in action and is required to present evidence of his/her coaching activities to an NVQ-approved assessor, who in most cases will also be a senior coach from the National Governing Body.

The form of evidence required as proof of competence will depend upon the sport and the level of the award. This will take the form of seeing the coach in action, or simulated exercises, plus a combination of all or some of the following: written logbooks or case studies, oral presentations, and/or portfolios of evidence of prior achievements such as videos, certificates and test results. Coaches who wish to present themselves for assessment need to start to keep detailed records of their activities as proof of actual coach expertise.

Candidates can start at any level, depending on the level of responsibility in their job, and can work their way up to level 4 or eventually 5. To date, S/NVQs in coaching are available at Level 2 in twenty-five sports, with some sports offering Level 4. NGBs will have information on approved centres that make assessments on their behalf.

## Sports Policy

Since the publication of *Sport: Raising the Game* by the Department of National Heritage in 1995 there has been a shift in sports policy towards performance and excellence. In his introduction, the Prime Minister, John Major, highlighted the importance of success in international competition. Although the 'sports development continuum' (Foundation, Participation, Performance and Excellence) recognizes the interdependence between 'grass-roots' and elite sport, the balance has shifted away from 'Sport for All' towards achieving excellence in fewer, strategically selected sports.

Important factors in sports policy in the 1990s have been the advent of the National Lottery and the Sports Lottery Fund [SLF], and the reorganization of the GB Sports Council in 1996. There are now five national sports councils, one for each of the 'home countries' – England, Scotland, Northern Ireland and Wales – and the UK Sports Council. The latter's remit is to focus performance and excellence issues at UK level, to act as a co-ordinating body, including doping control, to deal with international relations, and to promote the UK as a venue for world-class events.

The Sports Councils implement strategic objectives through 'advocacy' (lobbying on behalf of sport), and working in partnership with other sports agencies such as national governing bodies, local authorities, local sports councils and clubs. They also use 'grant aid' leverage to increase the number and improve the quality of facilities across the range of sports. There is a clear link between improving facilities, coach development, and recognizing and nurturing sporting talent. All of these objectives require financial support.

Coach- and athlete-centred funding programmes have begun to emerge through changes to the Sports Lottery Fund Revenue programmes, and these are essential if sports policies are to be turned into results on the world stage. In order to benefit from the additional resources from the National Lottery that are supporting sport in the UK a certain amount of administrative effort is required. Although the 'better bidder' is not always the most deserving, it is worth remembering that the distribution agencies can only give funds to those organizations and individuals that apply.

Striving to reach higher competitive levels is a very difficult business. Greater rewards and recognition drive more performers to try and emulate our current superstars. Further, not only is the competition stronger, but the level of achievement required to become nationally recognized is increasingly demanding. In the face of these related challenges, forward-thinking performers will look to assemble the best support system available to gain the competitive edge required. Being open-minded and ready to borrow useful ideas from many external influences seems to have helped our very best performers in the past, and this policy still holds true as the millenium beckons. Clearly these services will be integral to the development of our best young performers in the future.

## A Personal Developmental Process for Sport

Children can best be helped to gain competence and satisfaction through sport by supportive coaches and parents having a fuller understanding of the nature of the changes they experience. As we have already seen, they grow and mature (in a psychological, physical and emotional sense) at times and rates which are predetermined. From this we can map out distinct general phases of their young lives as they relate to greater involvement in sporting activity. This is useful in that it provides a template for matching ability, readiness and sport development in a way which is not traditionally presented to those directly involved. We have tried to present what is quite a complex process in an easily understood way for pleasurable and successful achievement in sport.

From this holistic perspective, nine key stages emerge and are presented below. It is important that an overall understanding of this process precedes a more specialized knowledge of particular parts or phases. In this way it is possible to stand back from direct involvement at one point in time to see how the lifelong picture is likely to unfold.

This may lead coaches to see themselves as only one, albeit an important, developer of potential along with a chain of other supporters at different developmental points in time. This is helpful in that it focuses attention on the needs of the performer as being paramount. The role of the coach may be in the early pre-school foundation stage, or it might be at the other end of the chain, working with elite performers. Both are critical to the development of the child. If this process is to happen smoothly, coaches need to recognize their own limitations and be ready to pass an athlete on to someone else at a mutually agreed point to facilitate further improvement.

Moreover, it is also important to see the coaching process as a long-term, slowly developing relationship where gradual change in ability will predominate. Knowing how performers develop should impact upon planning, practice selection and expectations of performer success. Knowing what challenges are ahead will ensure that more specialized work is introduced at the time of greatest readiness for maximum success.

For parents, a better understanding of the process of change is often hard to imagine when fully involved in the minutiae of everyday life. However, an awareness of the process presents certain advantages. It helps to understand what practitioners are working towards and creates opportunities to be supportive of their efforts. It allows for more appropriate decision-making about selecting activity, coaches and equipment whilst also identifying when a change is required just before boredom and dissatisfaction appear. Most importantly, it can demonstrate exactly what sport can and should offer regardless of the parent's own past sporting experiences. The notion of being physically literate, initially for its own sake and then as the means of stimulating cognitive processing is not widely appreciated. Similarly, the need to present children with problem-solving challenges and to develop skills in a variety of situations is a valuable life skill across different settings. Both of these issues suggest that there may well be more to sport than most parents think. So let us look more closely as the processes involved.

## Initiation (0–6 years)

Involves the interlinked processes of Observation, Exploration and Manipulation.

1. Observation: infants watch their world, and the people in it, in order to make sense of their place. Providing opportunities to watch stimulating activities should come first. Parents play a critical part in ensuring that infant's first life experiences are positive, varied and presented in a non-judgmental way. The choice of what is seen lies firmly with the parent, relative or carer at this point and so it is important that the right balance is achieved between the types of objects, activities and experiences which are introduced. All are equally valuable provided they are appropriate to an infant's sensory ability.

2. Exploration: the need to discover new and more stimulating environments

motivates the individual to develop movement and communication skills. Whilst the adult is still largely in control of the immediate environment, the infant can now make simple choices as to what is initially more worthy of their attention. Their positive reaction to new stimuli they have discovered is the main aim and their pleasure will lead to repetition of enjoyable activities and make them more adventurous. This in turn provides a need to become more mobile, which is a combination of strength, co-ordination and balance. This is the starting point for all motor movements, which are then refined into the various skills such as running, climbing and balancing.

3.   Manipulation: the physical organization of child-sized objects to stimulate thought processes and creativity. Periods of play become extended, as children become increasingly adept and dextrous. They also invent games, which allow practice of recently acquired ability, often mimicking home, and school, scenarios. This concept of manipulation also refers to children becoming more able to control their movements and transfer them to challenging situations, such as moving bouncing skills from a bed to a mini trampoline. They quickly learn to control themselves in time and space. The adult role is to present small progressive challenges, which further develop their self-esteem and personal achievement.

## Participation ( 7–13 years )

Involves repeated involvement in activity through Generalization, Integration and movement towards Specialization.

4.   Generalization: children's desire to express themselves through the attainment of generalized sports movement skills at a time when growth rates slow down. This is the starting point for sport for many children and is related to initial involvement in formalized activity. Extended opportunities arise from participation in Physical Education lessons and sports clubs which introduce mini versions of adult activity. Whilst  competing opportunities exist, parents need to consider their relative worth in terms of both the extent of involvement and the quality of those experiences.

5.   Integration: when general abilities combine with fitness and mental control to allow more specialized games and activities to be successfully introduced to children. Children start to choose role models, often in sport, and begin evaluating their ability relative to their friends. Coaches need to structure activity to maximize personal success from optimal involvement. Children's increased desire to learn leads them to consider a wide range of competing activities, not all of which could be as useful a vehicle for life as sport. Children can also learn skills in one sports setting and integrate them into another. For example, a basic skill such as running can be used in a variety of ways in football, or transferred to running on a track.

6.   Specialization: when the desire to follow a particular sporting activity leads to the decision to train, work with a coach and compete with serious intention. From late childhood to adolescence, children opt out of things to which they are not suited, on the basis of their perception of personal competence. This occurs at a time of considerable personal development during  puberty when ability, self-confidence and attitude tend to ebb and flow. Having reduced the number of areas of personal interest, they start to decide how much time to devote to each selected activity, sometimes on the basis of how much pleasure it brings or how good they think they might become.

## Continuation (13 years onwards)

The final performance stage links realization of ability with maintenance of interest and a healthy lifestyle, providing the child continues in sport.

7.   Realization: when self confidence from physical maturity, emotional stability and co-ordinated support systems sufficiently raises the level of performance recognition to the extent that going further in sport becomes a realistic option. The benefits of sport, whatever the level, become clearer. Those who wish to maintain their involvement without the competitive pressures of elite commitment will still gain huge benefits from participation. These can include improved physical health, good opportunities for social interaction and a safe and/or productive way to spend their free time. A message to parents to encourage and support their children regardless of ability is critical to their overall development.

   For the few who have the ability to aspire to the highest levels of achievement, now is the time when lifestyle decisions have to be fully considered. In order for this potential to be realized, the child will have to commit to the sport at the expense of a 'normal' teenage existence. Careful planning is the key to success.

   This long-term plan should consist of simple steps that provide developmentally related activity in a progressive way. Having a plan leaves less to chance and also reduces the chances of performer burnout as a result of doing too much, which may be too difficult, too soon. It also allows those who support talented youngsters to become more involved as they better understand the process and their own contribution to it. This cannot be achieved without a fully supportive family, an understanding school and a child who is prepared to work harder than ever before.

8.   Termination: some sports appear to have a short shelf life in that competitors start young and finish their careers at a very early age. In gymnastics, for example, a competitor may retire at fifteen years of age having reached the pinnacle of a career representing at least ten years of heavy involvement. In contrast, a javelin thrower may not start serious training until a year later and peak in his mid-thirties. However, retirement from competitive sport is an inevitable

conclusion and one best prepared for. For athletes who have spent a significant part of their life in a competitive sport, retirement can be a huge problem. Feelings of depression and loss similar to the grief process are often in evidence. The more balanced an athlete's life is outside the sport, the easier retirement becomes. Coaches can become proactive in this process, showing athletes that it is not the end, but merely a time for a positive change.

9.    Transformation: this stage of the process can be different for each individual. Those involved in sports which peak at any early age could consider using their skills in alternative sports. A female gymnast may have appropriate training for successful transfer to pole vault, or a swimmer might combine his former skills to meet the challenge of the triathlon. Athletes should strongly consider continued involvement rather than think that their only option is to withdraw completely from competitive sport.

Another option is for athletes to transform themselves into coaches. All sports have coach training schemes available which athletes can become involved in from late adolescence. This gives them the option to remain actively involved and use their recent competitive experience to benefit the next generation. Their relative inexperience should not preclude them from initial involvement. All sports need young, enthusiastic coaches if the sport is to develop and progress.

The stages outlined above represent our view of an appropriate development through sport. We have adopted this developmental perspective in order to demonstrate the different role that sport has to play in a child's life in accordance with their maturity. This book stresses the need for coaches and parents to be fully cognisant of the issues as a prerequisite for the children to have as rich and fulfilling an experience of sport as possible. It is only when there are positive partnerships that the child receives an enhanced life through sport. If we are to ensure a healthy and active population in the new millennium, it is essential that these ideas are taken on board.

We believe that children who have enjoyed pleasurable participation in sport will lead enhanced lives as adults; surely this is something we want for all our children.

# Further Reading

Black, J., *Mindstore* (Thorsons, 1994)

Britton, L., *Montessori*: Play and Learn (Vermilion, 1992)

Bull, S., *Sport Psychology – A Self-Help Guide* (The Crowood Press, 1992)

Butler, R., *Sports Psychology in Performance* (Butterworth Heinemann, 1997)

Dintiman, G., *Sports Speed* (Human Kinetics, 1997)

Gawain, S., *Living in the Light* (Bantam Books, 1993)

Haywood, K., *Life Span Motor Development* (Human Kinetics, 1993)

Hazeldine, R., *Strength Training for Sport* (The Crowood Press, 1993)

Lee, M., *Coaching Children in Sport* (E&FN Spon, 1993)

Malina, R., *Growth, Maturation and Physical Activity* (Human Kinetics, 1991)

Miller, B., *Gold Minds* (The Crowood Press, 1997)

NCF, *The Successful Coach* (NCF, 1996)

Norris, C., *Flexibility – Principles and Practice* (A&C Black, 1995)

Orlick, T. & Botterill, C., *Every Kid Can Win* (Nelson Hall, 1980)

Paish, W., *Training for Peak Performance* (A&C Black, 1991)

Price, S., *Aromatherapy for Common Ailments* (Gaia Books, 1991)

Raeburn, P., *Training for Speed and Endurance* (Allen & Unwin, 1996)

Rotella, R. & Bunker, L., *Parenting Your Superstar* (Leisure Press, 1987)

Smith, B., *Flexibility for Sport* (The Crowood Press, 1994)

Smoll, F. et al., *Children in Sport* (Human Kinetics, 1988)

Wilson, P., *Instant Calm* (Penguin, 1995)

# Useful Contacts

British Association of Sport and Exercise Sciences: 01132 78411
British Olympic Association: 0181 871 2677
Childline: 0800 1111
Foundation for Sport and the Arts: 0151 524 0235
National Sports Medicine Institute: 0171 251 0583
NCF: 01132 744802
Northern Ireland Sports Council: 01232 382222
Running Sport (Sports Administration): 0171 273 1737
Scottish Sports Council: 0131 339 9000
Sport England Lottery Helpline: 0345 649649
Sports Aid Foundation: 0171 387 9380
Sportspages (Sports Bookshop): 0171 240 9604
SPRITO (NVQs): 0171 388 7755
Welsh Sports Council: 01222 300500
Women's Sport Foundation: 0171 831 7863

# Index